Globalization and Sashetization Effects

Globalization and Sashetization Effects

Rafeal Mechlore

UNIEK ENTERPRISES

CONTENTS

INDEX

Chapter6Case Studies

Chapter7Challenges and Controversies

Chapter8Opportunities and Solutions

Chapter9Future Trends and Prospects

INDRODUCION

In a time characterized by extraordinary interconnectedness, the world is seeing the significant and frequently confusing impacts of two strong powers: globalization and sashetization. These two ideas, while particular, are inseparably connected, molding the manner in which we live, work, consume, and collaborate on a worldwide scale. In this book, we leave on an excursion to disentangle the complex elements of these peculiarities and grasp their sweeping outcomes on culture, financial matters, innovation, and society.

Globalization, a term that has become omnipresent in scholar, political, and public talk, connotes the steadily extending reliance and mix of countries, societies, economies, and individuals across the globe. This many-sided snare of associations is driven by a bunch of elements, remembering progresses for correspondence and transportation, the progression of exchange and money, and the persevering walk of mechanical development. Globalization has, on one hand, opened up new skylines of chance, encouraging financial development, social trade, and the free progression of thoughts. Then again, it has produced huge difficulties, like pay imbalance, social homogenization, and ecological debasement.

Sashetization, while a less natural term, addresses an idea that has acquired conspicuousness as of late as a contradiction to globalization. It envelops the developing pattern of people and networks looking to protect, celebrate, and declare their extraordinary social characters even with globalizing powers. Sashetization appears in different structures, from a restoration of customary traditions and practices to the transformation of worldwide impacts into nearby settings. It is a reaction to the homogenizing propensities of globalization, driven by the craving to hold social legacy and state one's personality in a quickly impacting world.

The crash and cooperative energy of globalization and sashetization are at the core of our investigation. While globalization encourages the progression of thoughts, items, and innovations across borders, sashetization typifies the reaction to these streams, as social orders look to keep up with their uniqueness and legitimacy. A complex and developing exchange brings up issues about the idea of personality, the elements of force, and the way ahead in this present reality where borders, both physical and social, are turning out to be progressively permeable.

Reason and Meaning of the Book

This book looks to dive profoundly into the mind boggling connection among globalization and sashetization, giving a thorough examination of their belongings and cooperations across different spaces. Our point is to reveal insight into the multi-layered results of these powers, drawing according to interdisciplinary viewpoints and certifiable contextual analyses.

As a matter of some importance, this investigation is opportune and huge because of the groundbreaking idea of globalization and the rising conspicuousness of sashetization as a reaction. As we stand at the crossing point of these worldwide patterns, understanding their consequences for different parts of our lives is basic. Whether one is a policymaker exploring the difficulties of a globalized economy, a business chief looking to venture into new business sectors, or a singular wrestling with inquiries of character and social legacy, this book offers important bits of knowledge.

Besides, this work highlights the significance of cultivating exchange and grasping between various societies and social orders. It perceives the requirement for capable and moral ways to deal with globalization that recognize the variety and extravagance of human societies. By looking at the effects of sashetization, we gain a more profound appreciation for the strength of social personalities and the creative manners by which they adjust to evolving conditions.

Outline of Parts

Part I: Prologue to Globalization and Sashetization

This section, which you are as of now perusing, gives an outline of the book's targets, the meaning of the subject, and the design of resulting parts.

Figuring out Globalization

Here, we dive into the authentic advancement of globalization, recognizing key drivers, speculations, and contemporary patterns. This central comprehension will act as a reason for understanding its connection with sashetization.

Part III: Sashetization: Idea and Setting

This part investigates the idea of sashetization inside and out, following its starting points and rise, and inspecting its social, financial, and innovative aspects.

Part IV: Globalization's Effect on Sashetization

We research what globalization means for sashetization, investigating social homogenization, monetary open doors and difficulties, mechanical network, and the social and natural outcomes of these elements.

Sashetization's Impact on Globalization

This part moves the concentration to how sashetization, as a reaction to globalization, impacts worldwide cycles. We analyze how customer conduct, market extension methodologies, advancement, and social trade are formed by sashetization.

Contextual investigations

Through true contextual analyses, we give substantial instances of how globalization and sashetization communicate in various settings, from arising economies to worldwide brands and the domain of innovation.

Difficulties and Discussions

We basically dissect the difficulties and contentions emerging from the crash of globalization and sashetization, including social assignment, pay disparity, innovative reliance, and natural effects.

Part VIII: Open doors and Arrangements

In this part, we investigate open doors and expected arrangements, including advancing social trade, feasible sashetization rehearses, moral globalization drives, and strategy suggestions.

Future Patterns and Prospects

We look into the future, taking into account how globalization and sashetization could develop, analyzing the job of arising innovations, supportability concerns, worldwide administration, and offering expectations and hypotheses.

1

Chapter1

Introduction

In a period characterized by uncommon interconnectedness, the world is seeing the significant and frequently dumbfounding impacts of two strong powers: globalization and sashetization. These two ideas, while unmistakable, are inseparably connected, molding the manner in which we live, work, consume, and communicate on a worldwide scale. In this book, we leave on an excursion to unwind the mind boggling elements of these peculiarities and figure out their broad results on culture, financial matters, innovation, and society.

Globalization and Its Multi-layered Effect

Globalization, a term that has become pervasive in scholar, political, and public talk, implies the steadily growing relationship and combination of countries, societies, economies, and individuals across the globe. This complicated trap of associations is driven by a horde of variables, remembering progresses for correspondence and transportation, the progression of exchange and money, and the determined walk of mechanical development. Globalization has, on one hand, opened up new skylines of chance, encouraging financial development, social trade, and the free progression of thoughts. Then again, it has created critical difficulties, like pay disparity, social homogenization, and natural debasement.

The verifiable development of globalization is a demonstration of its groundbreaking power. While the underlying foundations of globalization can be followed back to old shipping lanes, the peculiarity as far as we might be concerned today has been formed by floods of mechanical development and international movements. The time of investigation and expansionism in the fifteenth to eighteenth hundreds of years, for example, saw the spread of merchandise, societies, and thoughts across mainlands. In the nineteenth hundred years, the Modern Unrest achieved propels in transportation and correspondence, making way for the cutting edge time of globalization. Quick forward to the late twentieth and mid 21st hundreds of years, and we end up in a world

portrayed by momentary correspondence, worldwide stockpile chains, and transnational organizations.

Globalization is definitely not a solid power; rather, it includes a range of aspects, from monetary and social to political and natural. Monetarily, globalization has worked with the development of merchandise, administrations, and capital across borders, setting out open doors for organizations to extend their business sectors and for purchasers to get to a more extensive scope of items. Socially, it has prompted a rich embroidery of multifaceted trade, where thoughts, craftsmanship, music, and cooking rise above topographical limits. Strategically, globalization has provoked the development of worldwide associations, arrangements, and arrangements that look to oversee worldwide issues and advance participation. Earth, it has raised complex difficulties, as the worldwide development of products and the utilization of assets strain the planet's environments.

However, for all its extraordinary potential, globalization has not been without its faultfinders and cynics. The financial advantages have not been equally disseminated, with numerous districts and networks encountering position removal, wage stagnation, and monetary unsteadiness. Social globalization, while encouraging variety, has additionally raised worries about the disintegration of neighborhood customs and personalities. Natural globalization has added to environmental emergencies, including environmental change and asset exhaustion. Political globalization has confronted opposition from the people who view it as subverting public power and a vote based system.

Sashetization: A Reaction to Globalization

Enter sashetization, a term that, while a less recognizable idea, addresses a basic reaction to the homogenizing propensities of globalization. Sashetization envelops the developing pattern of people and networks trying to save, celebrate, and attest their special social characters notwithstanding globalizing powers. It is a reaction portrayed by a well established want to shield social legacy, keep up with uniqueness, and state one's personality in a quickly impacting world.

Sashetization appears in different structures, from a restoration of conventional traditions and practices to the variation of worldwide impacts into neighborhood settings. It is, at its center, a unique cycle that perceives the significance of legacy, custom, and social personality in our current reality where globalization can possibly dissolve these establishments.

Grasping the Transaction Among Globalization and Sashetization

The impact and collaboration of globalization and sashetization are at the core of our investigation. These two powers are not really restricting; all things considered, they coincide and connect in complex ways. Globalization cultivates the progression of thoughts, items, and innovations across borders, making a worldwide town where data goes at the speed of light, and societies interlace. Sashetization, thusly, typifies the reaction to these streams, as social orders look to keep up with their peculiarity and credibility in a globalized world.

The exchange among globalization and sashetization is much the same as a fragile dance, where societies get, adjust, and develop while holding their center personality. A complex and developing collaboration brings up issues about the idea of personality, the elements of force, and the way ahead in reality as we know it where borders, both physical and social, are turning out to be progressively permeable.

In this book, we embrace an extensive assessment of the impacts of globalization and sashetization on different features of our inter-connected world. We will investigate the unpredictable connection between these peculiarities, giving significant experiences to policymakers, business pioneers, researchers, and people the same.

Reason and Meaning of the Book

The motivation behind this book is to give a profound and nuanced comprehension of the mind boggling interchange among globalization and sashetization and to explain their impacts on culture, financial matters, innovation, and society. Our point is to add to the continuous talk on these worldwide patterns and their suggestions for a quickly impacting world.

This investigation is ideal and huge because of the groundbreaking idea of globalization and the rising noticeable quality of sashetization as a reaction. As we stand at the convergence of these worldwide patterns, understanding their impacts on different parts of our lives is basic. Whether one is a policymaker exploring the difficulties of a globalized economy, a business chief looking to venture into new business sectors, or a singular wrestling with inquiries of character and social legacy, this book offers important experiences.

Besides, this work highlights the significance of cultivating discourse and figuring out between various societies and social orders. It perceives the requirement for mindful and moral ways to deal with globalization that recognize the variety and extravagance of human societies. By looking at the effects of sashetization, we gain a more profound appreciation for the flexibility of social personalities and the creative manners by which they adjust to evolving conditions.

Outline of Parts

Section I: Prologue to Globalization and Sashetization

This section, which you are at present perusing, gives an outline of the book's targets, the meaning of the point, and the construction of resulting parts.

Section II: Figuring out Globalization

Here, we dive into the authentic advancement of globalization, recognizing key drivers, speculations, and contemporary patterns. This essential comprehension will act as a reason for understanding its connection with sashetization.

Section III: Sashetization: Idea and Setting

This part investigates the idea of sashetization top to bottom, following its beginnings and rise, and inspecting its social, financial, and mechanical aspects.

Part IV: Globalization's Effect on Sashetization

We research what globalization means for sashetization, investigating social homogenization, monetary open doors and difficulties, mechanical network, and the social and ecological results of these elements.

Section V: Sashetization's Impact on Globalization

This section moves the concentration to how sashetization, as a reaction to globalization, impacts worldwide cycles. We look at how shopper conduct, market extension procedures, development, and social trade are formed by sashetization.

Section VI: Contextual investigations

Through true contextual analyses, we give substantial instances of how globalization and sashetization communicate in various settings, from arising economies to worldwide brands and the domain of innovation.

Section VII: Difficulties and Debates

We basically break down the difficulties and discussions emerging from the crash of globalization and sashetization, including social appointment, pay imbalance, mechanical reliance, and natural effects.

Section VIII: Potential open doors and Arrangements

In this section, we investigate valuable open doors and expected arrangements, including advancing social trade, reasonable sashetization rehearses, moral globalization drives, and strategy suggestions.

Section IX: Future Patterns and Prospects

We look into the future, taking into account how globalization and sashetization could develop, inspecting the job of arising innovations, manageability concerns, worldwide administration, and offering forecasts and hypotheses.

1.1 Definition of Globalization

Meaning of Globalization

Globalization is a multi-layered and complex peculiarity that has been molding the world in significant ways for quite a long time. A term frequently shows up in conversations across different fields, including financial matters, governmental issues, culture, and innovation. Notwithstanding, showing up at an exact and generally acknowledged meaning of globalization can be trying because of its different indications and continuous development. In this part, we will investigate the idea of globalization, its key aspects, and the different ways it is perceived and depicted.

1. The Complex Idea of Globalization

At its center, globalization alludes to the rising interconnectedness and association of countries and people groups across the globe. It includes a large number of cycles, cooperations, and patterns that rise above public limits. While globalization is frequently connected with monetary factors, for example, exchange and money, a multi-layered peculiarity reaches out to different parts of human existence. These aspects include:

1. **Financial Globalization:** This aspect centers around the incorporation of public economies into a solitary worldwide commercial center. It includes the development of products, administrations,

capital, and data across borders. Monetary globalization is described by the advancement of exchange, the ascent of worldwide companies, and the rise of worldwide inventory chains.

2. **Social Globalization:** Social globalization includes the trade and scattering of thoughts, values, rehearses, and social items (e.g., music, films, style) on a worldwide scale. It frequently prompts the mixing and hybridization of societies as individuals from various foundations communicate and impact each other.

3. **Political Globalization:** Political globalization alludes to the rising interconnectedness of political frameworks and the development of worldwide administration structures. Worldwide associations, deals, and arrangements represent this aspect as they look to address worldwide difficulties, for example, environmental change, common liberties, and security.

4. **Mechanical Globalization:** Advances in correspondence and data advances play had a significant impact in globalization. The web, cell phones, and computerized stages have worked with immediate worldwide correspondence, data sharing, and the rise of a worldwide advanced economy.

5. **Social Globalization:** Social globalization relates to the interconnectedness of people and networks around the world. It includes worldwide relocation, the spread of social developments, and the worldwide dispersion of information and instruction.

2. Meanings of Globalization

1. **Monetary Viewpoint:**

"Globalization is the course of association and reconciliation among individuals, organizations, and state run administrations of various countries, driven by worldwide exchange and venture and supported by data innovation." - IMF (Worldwide Money related Asset)

"Globalization is the overall peculiarity of mechanical, financial, political, and social trades, achieved by current correspondence, transportation, and legitimate foundation, as well as the political decision to deliberately open cross-line joins in worldwide exchange and money." - Harvard College

2. **Social Point of view:**
"Globalization alludes to the escalation of social and financial relations among people groups and nations." - Arjun Appadurai, Anthropologist

"Globalization is the unyielding joining of business sectors, country states, and innovations to a degree never saw — in a manner that is empowering people, enterprises, and country states to stretch all over the planet farther, quicker, more profound, and less expensive than at any other time." - Thomas L. Friedman, Columnist and Creator

3. **Political Viewpoint:**

"Globalization is the cycle by which occasions, choices, and exercises in a single region of the planet can come to have critical ramifications for people and networks in very far off pieces of the globe." - David Held, Political Specialist

"Globalization is the strengthening of overall social relations that connect far off territories so that neighborhood happenings are formed by occasions happening somewhere far off as well as the other way around." - Anthony Giddens, Humanist

3. **Key Components of Globalization**

Interconnectedness: Globalization includes the production of organizations and linkages that interface people, associations, and countries across topographical limits. These organizations work with the trading of products, administrations, data, and thoughts.

Relationship: Globalization prompts expanded association among nations and locales. Monetary and political choices in a single area of the planet can have sweeping consequences for different locales, making countries dependent on each other.

Incorporation: Globalization involves the coordination of economies, societies, and social orders. This combination can bring about both positive results, like expanded exchange and social trade, and difficulties, like social homogenization and financial disparity.

Speed and Availability: Advances in innovation have sped up the speed of globalization. Data and information can be sent across the globe progressively, working with fast direction and worldwide joint effort.

Change: Globalization can possibly change social orders, economies, and political frameworks. It can prompt monetary development, social variety, and the spread of vote based values. Nonetheless, it can likewise add to imbalance, social conflicts, and ecological debasement.

4. Developing Nature of Globalization

It is urgent to perceive that globalization is certainly not a static peculiarity however a continuous interaction. After some time, the nature and effect of globalization have developed, molded by evolving innovative, monetary, political, and social variables. For instance, the globalization of the late twentieth 100 years and mid 21st hundred years, frequently alluded to as "globalization 2.0," was portrayed by the quick development of computerized advances and the rise of worldwide stock chains.

Today, we are seeing the proceeded with development of globalization, frequently alluded to as "globalization 3.0" or the "Fourth Modern Unrest." This stage is set apart by advancements in computerized reasoning, mechanization, and the Web of Things (IoT), which are reshaping enterprises, work markets, and correspondence on a worldwide scale. Besides, the Coronavirus pandemic has featured both the weaknesses and versatility of worldwide frameworks, provoking a reassessment of globalization's elements.

1.2 Definition of Sashetization

Sashetization is a somewhat late idea that catches a critical cultural reaction to the powers of globalization. While not quite so generally perceived as globalization, sashetization addresses a significant offset to the homogenizing inclinations of worldwide interconnectedness. This term exemplifies the developing pattern of people, networks, and, surprisingly, whole countries trying to save, celebrate, and state their one of a kind social characters despite globalizing powers. To completely comprehend sashetization, we should investigate its definition, setting, and the variables that drive this peculiarity.

1. **The Pith of Sashetization**

   At its center, sashetization alludes to the cognizant work to shield, rejuvenate, and advance social legacy, customs, and uniqueness. This reaction emerges from a firmly established want to keep up with social personality and credibility in a quickly impacting world described by globalization. Sashetization incorporates different features, including:

   Social Conservation: The safeguarding of customary traditions, ceremonies, dialects, and imaginative articulations. This might include endeavors to archive and communicate social information to people in the future.

   Social Recovery: The resurgence of social practices and customs that might have been minimized or dissolved over the long haul. Networks might resuscitate conventional celebrations, artworks, or dialects that were near the precarious edge of annihilation.

   Social Transformation: The consolidation of worldwide impacts into nearby settings while keeping up with center social qualities. This transformation should be visible in different perspectives, from cooking and style to music and craftsmanship.

   Social Attestation: The statement of social personality and pride, frequently because of outer tensions or social homogenization. This might incorporate endeavors to oppose digestion and declare the uniqueness of one's way of life.

   Sashetization is, subsequently, a dynamic and complex reaction that can show distinctively in different locales and among various networks. It encapsulates a guarantee to saving social variety and opposing the disintegration of social personalities in a globalized world.

2. The Setting of Sashetization

Globalization: The general setting for sashetization is globalization itself. The expanded progression of data, thoughts, and social items across boundaries can prompt a feeling of social homogenization, where worldwide impacts rule neighborhood customs. Sashetization fills in as a reaction to this pattern.

Mechanical Advances: Advances in correspondence innovation, especially the web and online entertainment, have made it more straightforward for people and networks to associate with similar individuals all over the planet who share an interest in saving their social legacy.

Relocation and Diaspora: The development of individuals across borders, whether because of financial reasons, struggle, or different variables, frequently prompts the protection and transformation of social customs in new conditions. Diaspora people group can assume a critical part in sashetization endeavors.

Social Colonialism: The insight that predominant worldwide societies, frequently spread by media and global organizations, take steps to eclipse neighborhood societies can spike sashetization. This should be visible in protection from the spread of Western shopper culture, for instance.

Political and Social Developments: Sashetization can be interwoven with political and social developments pushing for social privileges, native freedoms, or independence. These developments frequently look to secure and advance the social legacy of minimized networks.

3. Sashetization and Social Character

Key to the idea of sashetization is the possibility of social personality. Social character includes the convictions, values, practices, and customs that characterize a specific gathering or local area. It is a wellspring of pride, having a place, and union, furnishing people with a feeling of shared history and legacy.

Sashetization is driven by the acknowledgment that social personality isn't static; it advances and adjusts over the long run. In any case, even with globalization's fast changes and the expected disintegration of neighborhood customs, there is a craving to protect the center components that make a culture one of a kind.

Social character isn't just a natural part of individual and local area personality however can likewise have more extensive social and political ramifications. It can impact social attachment, intergroup relations, and, surprisingly, political developments looking for social independence or acknowledgment. Consequently, sashetization assumes a fundamental part in the continuous talk about the significance of social variety in an interconnected world.

4. **Instances of Sashetization**

Language Rejuvenation: Native people group in many regions of the planet are attempting to renew jeopardized dialects. Endeavors incorporate language drenching programs, recording oral chronicles, and advancing the utilization of local dialects in schooling.

Social Celebrations: People group frequently sort out social celebrations and occasions to praise their customs and legacy. These occasions give potential chances to individuals to associate with their social roots and offer their legacy with others.

Culinary Practices: Food is a strong articulation of culture. Numerous people group invest wholeheartedly in safeguarding and sharing customary recipes and cooking procedures, even as they adjust to present day preferences and fixings.

Customary Dress: Conventional apparel and clothing can be a significant image of social character. Endeavors to keep up with and adjust customary dress styles are a typical part of sashetization.

Social Training: Instructive establishments and local area associations assume a part in showing social customs to new ages. This incorporates music, dance, makes, and narrating.

5. Sashetization and Worldwide Cooperation

One could contemplate whether sashetization goes against the standards of globalization, given its accentuation on saving social peculiarity. Nonetheless, sashetization isn't intrinsically noninterventionist or gone against to worldwide

collaboration. All things being equal, it addresses a nuanced reaction to globalization, perceiving that social variety is a fundamental piece of the worldwide mosaic.

Sashetization can exist together with globalization in more than one way:

Social Trade: Sashetization doesn't block social trade. Truth be told, it frequently includes the dynamic imparting of social practices to other people who appreciate and regard those customs.

Hybridization: While sashetization tries to protect center social components, it can likewise include the transformation of worldwide impacts in manners that line up with nearby qualities and practices. This can bring about social hybridization, where new social articulations arise.

Worldwide Organizations: Sashetization endeavors can profit from worldwide organizations and joint efforts. The web, for example, empowers similar people and gatherings to associate and share encounters, systems, and assets for social protection.

1.3 Purpose and Significance of the Book

The book "Globalization and Sashetization Impacts" fills in as a thorough investigation of the complicated elements among globalization and sashetization, revealing insight into their broad outcomes on culture, financial matters, innovation, and society. In this part, we dig into the particular reason and meaning of this book, featuring its significance in the contemporary world.

1. **Grasping the Interchange Among Globalization and Sashetization**

   Reason: The basic role of this book is to give perusers a profound and nuanced comprehension of how globalization and sashetization interface and impact one another. It looks to unwind the intricacies of these worldwide peculiarities and their consequences for different parts of our interconnected world.

   Globalization, with its multi-layered aspects, has reshaped the worldwide scene in significant ways. It has opened up valuable open doors for monetary development, social trade, and innovative headway, while likewise acting difficulties such like pay imbalance and social homogenization. Sashetization, as a reaction to globalization, addresses a cognizant work to save social personality and peculiarity. By analyzing the

   transaction between these powers, perusers can acquire bits of knowledge into the elements molding our reality.

   Importance: Understanding the transaction among globalization and sashetization is of fundamental significance in this day and age. These powers are not secluded; they exist together and associate in complex ways. Policymakers, business pioneers, researchers, and people the same need to get a handle on the ramifications of this communication to settle on informed choices and explore the difficulties and open doors introduced by a globalized world.

   As countries and networks wrestle with inquiries of character, social safeguarding, financial turn of events, and natural supportability, this book offers a guide for understanding the powers at play. It reveals insight into what globalization and sashetization mean for social variety, monetary abberations, mechanical development, and social elements.

2. **Inspecting the Multi-faceted Impacts**

   Reason: This book plans to investigate the multi-faceted impacts of globalization and sashetization across different spaces. It goes past oversimplified accounts and digs into the complexities of how these peculiarities shape culture, financial aspects, innovation, and society.

Globalization's effect reaches out a long ways past financial matters; it impacts culture, governmental issues, and innovation. Essentially, sashetization isn't exclusively a social peculiarity yet has monetary, political, and social ramifications. By inspecting these impacts completely, the book gives an all encompassing perspective on the outcomes of globalization and sashetization.

Importance: The multi-faceted investigation of impacts is huge in light of the fact that it recognizes the intricacy of the worldwide scene. For policymakers, this far reaching viewpoint is important in creating approaches that advance maintainable financial development, social variety, and social value. Business pioneers can acquire experiences into market elements, buyer conduct, and advancement patterns. Researchers and scientists can draw from a rich embroidery of data to propel how they might interpret these worldwide patterns.

3. **Empowering Moral and Informed Globalization**

   Reason: Moral contemplations are key to the book's motivation. It tries to support mindful and moral ways to deal with globalization. By looking at the difficulties and contentions related with globalization and sashetization, the book gives an establishment to conversations on the most proficient method to explore the worldwide scene in an ethically and socially mindful way.

   Globalization can intensify pay imbalance, add to ecological debasement, and lead to social apportionment. Perceiving these difficulties is the most important phase in tending to them. The book gives a stage to examining arrangements and advancing moral practices that moderate these unfortunate results.

   Importance: In a period where moral contemplations are vital, the book fills in as an asset for people, associations, and legislatures looking to adjust their activities to capable worldwide practices. It urges perusers to fundamentally assess the effect of their choices and think about the more extensive cultural and natural ramifications of globalization.

4. **Encouraging Discourse and Understanding**

Reason: The book expects to cultivate exchange and grasping between various societies and social orders. It perceives the significance of recognizing and regarding the variety of human societies while exploring the globalized world. By introducing contextual investigations, strategy suggestions, and moral contemplations, the book gives a stage to helpful discussions on social trade, participation, and protection.

Importance: Cultivating discourse and understanding is of worldwide importance. In our current reality where societies progressively converge, regarding and valuing assorted points of view and customs is essential for advancing harmony, resilience, and collaboration. This book adds to the more extensive discussion on social trade, empowering perusers to embrace the lavishness of worldwide variety while protecting the honesty of individual societies.

5. **Planning for What's in store**

Reason: The book expects to outfit perusers with bits of knowledge into future patterns and prospects connected with globalization and sashetization. It investigates arising innovations, maintainability concerns, worldwide administration, and expectations for how these powers might advance.

The world is in a condition of steady change, with new innovations and international movements reshaping the worldwide scene. By analyzing the likely directions of globalization and sashetization, the book helps perusers expect and get ready for the difficulties and open doors that lie ahead.

Importance: Planning for what's in store is fundamental for people, organizations, and legislatures. The bits of knowledge gave in this book can direct essential preparation, strategy improvement, and development endeavors. By remaining informed about future patterns, perusers can situate themselves to adjust and flourish in a quickly changing worldwide climate.

1.4 Overview of Chapters

This book, "Globalization and Sashetization Impacts," sets out on an extensive investigation of the perplexing interaction among globalization and sashetization and their significant results on culture, financial matters, innovation, and society. The accompanying outline gives a brief look into the parts that structure the center of this edifying excursion.

Part I: Prologue to Globalization and Sashetization

The book opens with this essential part, which lays the preparation for the investigation ahead. It acquaints perusers with the ideas of globalization and sashetization and their importance in the present interconnected world. The section frames the book's targets, accentuates the significance of the point, and gives an outline of the resulting parts. Toward the finish of this section, perusers will have an unmistakable comprehension of the book's extension and reason.

Section II: Grasping Globalization

This section dives into the verifiable advancement of globalization, following its underlying foundations and inspecting its vital drivers and hypotheses. It gives a complete comprehension of the monetary, social, political, innovative, and social elements of globalization. Perusers will acquire bits of knowledge into how globalization has formed the world, from the time of investigation to the advanced period of quick worldwide correspondence and transnational partnerships.

Section III: Sashetization: Idea and Setting

Section III acquaints perusers with the idea of sashetization, investigating its development, authentic setting, and social, financial, and innovative aspects. It digs into the explanations for the ascent of sashetization, stressing its job as a reaction to the difficulties presented by globalization. This section establishes the groundwork for understanding sashetization as a dynamic and multi-layered peculiarity that envelops social conservation, restoration, variation, and statement.

Section IV: Globalization's Effect on Sashetization

Expanding on the comprehension of both globalization and sashetization, Section IV looks at what globalization means for sashetization. It investigates the impacts of globalization on social variety, monetary open doors and difficulties, innovative network, and social and natural elements. Perusers will acquire bits of knowledge into how globalization can both undermine and cultivate sashetization endeavors, prompting a nuanced comprehension of this many-sided relationship.

Section V: Sashetization's Impact on Globalization

In Section V, the center movements to how sashetization, as a reaction to globalization, impacts worldwide cycles. The part investigates how sashetization shapes shopper conduct, market extension techniques, advancement, and social trade. Perusers will find how neighborhood societies adjust and state their uniqueness on the worldwide stage, adding to an additional different and interconnected world.

Section VI: Contextual analyses

This section brings hypothesis into training by introducing certifiable contextual investigations that delineate the complicated interchange among globalization and sashetization. Perusers will travel through different settings, from arising economies to worldwide brands and the domain of innovation, to acquire a more profound comprehension of how these worldwide powers manifest in unambiguous situations. The contextual analyses give substantial instances of the difficulties and valuable open doors looked by people, networks, and associations in a globalized world.

Section VII: Difficulties and Debates

Section VII basically inspects the difficulties and debates emerging from the crash of globalization and sashetization. It resolves complex issues like social assignment, pay disparity, innovative reliance, and natural effects. Perusers will acquire experiences into the moral problems and strategy challenges presented by these worldwide patterns, featuring the requirement for capable and manageable methodologies.

Section VIII: Open doors and Arrangements

As a contradiction to the difficulties, Section VIII investigates valuable open doors and likely arrangements. It offers a structure for advancing social trade, economical sashetization rehearses, moral globalization drives, and strategy suggestions. Perusers will find significant methodologies for tending to the adverse results of globalization while saddling its positive viewpoints to support social orders around the world.

Section IX: Future Patterns and Prospects

Section IX projects a forward-looking look, taking into account how globalization and sashetization could develop from now on. It investigates the job of arising advancements, manageability concerns, worldwide administration, and offers forecasts and hypotheses about the direction of these worldwide powers. Perusers will acquire experiences into the potential situations that anticipate in a steadily impacting world.

2

Chapter2

Understanding Globalization

Globalization is a multi-layered and groundbreaking power that has reshaped our reality throughout the course of recent many years. A term pervades conversations in financial matters, legislative issues, culture, innovation, and numerous different circles of human action. To really accept the idea of globalization, one should dig into its intricacy, looking at its authentic roots, key aspects, drivers, and results. This exposition leaves on an excursion to comprehend globalization, offering a complete investigation of this mind boggling peculiarity and its broad consequences for the cutting edge world.

1. Verifiable Underlying foundations of Globalization

Globalization is certainly not a new turn of events; its foundations expand profound into history. Understanding its authentic setting gives important bits of knowledge into its contemporary appearances. A few key verifiable variables have added to the development of globalization:

1. **Exchange and Investigation:** One of the earliest types of globalization can be followed back to the Silk Street, associating

East and West, and the journeys of investigation by European countries in the fifteenth and sixteenth hundreds of years. These excursions prompted the trading of merchandise, thoughts, and societies across mainlands.

2. **Modern Transformation:** The Modern Unrest in the eighteenth and nineteenth hundreds of years denoted a huge defining moment in globalization. The large scale manufacturing of products, mechanical progressions, and the development of transportation networks worked with the development of merchandise and individuals on an extraordinary scale.

3. **Data and Correspondence:** The creation of the message, trailed by the phone, radio, and in the end the web, changed worldwide correspondence. These advancements sped up the progression of data and made immediate worldwide associations conceivable.

II. Key Components of Globalization

1. **Financial Globalization:** Monetary globalization includes the combination of public economies into a solitary worldwide commercial center. It is portrayed by the development of merchandise, administrations, capital, and data across borders. Key perspectives incorporate worldwide exchange, worldwide organizations, and worldwide stock chains.

2. **Social Globalization:** Social globalization alludes to the trade and dispersal of thoughts, values, rehearses, and social items on a worldwide scale. It frequently prompts the mixing and hybridization of societies as individuals from various foundations interface and impact each other.

3. **Political Globalization:** Political globalization relates to the rising interconnectedness of political frameworks and the development of worldwide administration structures. Worldwide associations, deals, and arrangements embody this aspect as they

look to address worldwide difficulties, for example, environmental change, basic freedoms, and security.

4. **Mechanical Globalization:** Advances in correspondence and data advances play had a significant impact in globalization. The web, cell phones, and computerized stages have worked with quick worldwide correspondence, data sharing, and the development of a worldwide advanced economy.

5. **Social Globalization:** Social globalization relates to the interconnectedness of people and networks around the world. It incorporates worldwide relocation, the spread of social developments, and the worldwide dissemination of information and training.

III. Drivers of Globalization

1. **Innovation:** Mechanical progressions, particularly in data and correspondence innovation (ICT), have been an essential driver of globalization. ICT has empowered the fast transmission of data, brought down correspondence costs, and extended worldwide availability.

2. **Exchange Progression:** Strategies that advance deregulation and lessen exchange hindrances have worked with the development of labor and products across borders. Economic deals and associations like the World Exchange Association (WTO) play had a pivotal impact in advancing exchange progression.

3. **Venture and Capital Streams:** The globalization of monetary business sectors and the simplicity of cross-line capital streams have expanded speculation open doors and prompted the incorporation of monetary frameworks. Worldwide partnerships put resources into assorted markets, cultivating worldwide monetary association.

4. **Transportation and Framework:** Further developed transportation foundation, including air travel and delivery, has diminished the expense and time expected to get merchandise and individuals

across mainlands. This has energized exchange and the travel industry.

5. **Political Elements:** Political choices and arrangements likewise shape globalization. Legislatures may effectively advance or restrain globalization through economic alliance, international strategy, and movement approaches.

IV. Outcomes of Globalization

1. **Financial Development:** Globalization can drive monetary development by opening up new business sectors and cultivating contest. It permits nations to spend significant time in the development of labor and products where they enjoy a relative benefit.

2. **Pay Disparity:** One of the most discussed outcomes of globalization is its effect on pay imbalance. While it has lifted millions out of destitution, it has additionally added to abundance incongruities, both inside and between nations.

3. **Social Trade:** Social globalization has prompted the trading of thoughts, workmanship, music, and food across borders. This social trade enhances social orders yet can likewise prompt social homogenization or social government.

4. **Mechanical Progression:** Globalization encourages innovative development by empowering the progression of thoughts and information. Cooperation on a worldwide scale has prompted forward leaps in fields like medication, innovation, and science.

5. **Ecological Effect:** The expanded development of merchandise and individuals has ecological results, including fossil fuel byproducts, deforestation, and abuse of normal assets. Maintainable globalization rehearses are important to address these difficulties.

V. Contentions Encompassing Globalization

1. **Social Homogenization:** Pundits contend that globalization can prompt the disintegration of neighborhood societies as world-wide impacts overwhelm. The spread of Western shopper culture is in many cases refered to for instance.

2. **Loss of Power:** A view globalization as a danger to public sway, as peaceful accords and associations can oblige a country's capacity to settle on free choices.

3. **Work and Laborers' Privileges:** Globalization has prompted the rethinking of occupations to nations with lower work costs. This has raised worries about specialists' privileges and employer stability in both created and non-industrial countries.

4. **Natural Debasement:** The quest for financial development and worldwide exchange can add to ecological corruption, prompting worries about manageability and environmental change.

5. **Monetary Emergencies:** Globalization has been related with monetary emergencies, for example, the Asian monetary emergency of the last part of the 1990s and the worldwide monetary emergency of 2008. These emergencies have brought up issues about the soundness of the worldwide monetary framework.

VI. The Continuous Development of Globalization

It is critical to perceive that globalization is definitely not a static peculiarity however a continuous cycle. After some time, it has developed in light of evolving mechanical, financial, political, and social variables. The late twentieth and mid 21st hundreds of years have been portrayed by what some allude to as "globalization 2.0," set apart by the quick extension of advanced innovations and the rise of worldwide stockpile chains.

Today, we are seeing the proceeded with development of globalization, frequently alluded to as "globalization 3.0" or the "Fourth Modern Unrest." This stage is described by advancements in man-made reasoning, robotization, and the Web of Things (IoT), which are reshaping ventures, work markets, and correspondence on a worldwide scale.

2.1 Historical Evolution of Globalization

Globalization is a mind boggling and diverse peculiarity that has a long and many-sided history. It isn't just a new turn of events but instead a cycle that has developed over hundreds of years, driven by different powers and molded by verifiable occasions. To comprehend globalization completely, it is fundamental to investigate its verifiable development, from its initial roots to its contemporary appearances. This paper brings a profound jump into the verifiable excursion of globalization, featuring key achievements and changes en route.

1. **Early Foundations of Globalization**
   1. **The Silk Street:** The Silk Street, laid out around the second century BCE, was an organization of shipping lanes that associated the East and West. It worked with the trading of products, thoughts, and societies across huge distances, from China to the Mediterranean.
   2. **Old Exchange Domains:** The ascent of strong realms, for example, the Roman Domain and the Han Tradition in China, assumed a critical part in advancing exchange and social trade. These realms made conditions for the progression of products and thoughts across borders.
   3. **Nautical Investigation:** Sea investigation in old times, similar to the journeys of the Phoenicians and the Polynesians, added to early globalization by growing exchange organizations and social dispersion across seas.

II. The Time of Investigation and Colonization (fifteenth seventeenth Hundreds of years)

1. **Columbus and the New World:** Christopher Columbus' journeys to the Americas opened up another time of worldwide trade, known as the Columbian Trade. It presented yields, creatures,

and societies from the Old World to the New World as well as the other way around.

2. **Development of Worldwide Shipping lanes:** The Time of Investigation prompted the foundation of worldwide shipping lanes, including the Atlantic slave exchange, which had significant financial and social results around the world.

3. **European Expansionism:** European frontier realms extended across the Americas, Africa, and Asia, bringing about the trading of products and societies, yet in addition the burden of provincial rule and abuse.

III. Industrialization and the nineteenth Hundred years

1. **Modern Unrest:** The Modern Transformation, which started in the late eighteenth hundred years in England and spread to different pieces of Europe and the US, changed assembling and transportation. It filled worldwide exchange and monetary development.

2. **Development of Worldwide Business sectors:** Further developed transportation advancements, like steamships and rail lines, empowered the development of

   merchandise and individuals on an uncommon scale. Worldwide business sectors extended, and the progression of products expanded.

3. **Spread of Western Qualities:** The spread of Western qualities, including a vote based system and independence, went with monetary globalization. Western belief systems affected political developments and establishments around the world.

IV. The twentieth 100 years and the Universal Conflicts

1. **Worldwide Incorporation:** The mid twentieth century saw expanded worldwide joining, set apart by the foundation of global

associations like the Class of Countries, which intended to advance collaboration and forestall struggle.

2. **Universal Conflicts:** The two Universal Conflicts upset globalization. The Second Great War prompted monetary separation and the breakdown of the worldwide highest quality level. The Second Great War brought about broad obliteration and the division of the world into two superpower alliances during the Virus War.

V. Post-The Second Great War Time

1. **Bretton Woods Gathering:** The Bretton Woods Meeting in 1944 laid out another worldwide money related framework, cultivating monetary steadiness and working with post-war reproduction.

2. **The Assembled Countries:** The Assembled Countries (UN) was established in 1945 to advance harmony and global collaboration. It turned into a gathering for resolving worldwide issues and clashes.

3. **Ascent of Worldwide Partnerships:** The post-war time saw the quick development of global companies, which assumed a focal part in worldwide exchange and speculation.

VI. Contemporary Globalization

1. **Data Innovation Transformation:** The ascent of data innovation, especially the web and computerized correspondence, changed worldwide availability. It empowered moment correspondence and information trade on a worldwide scale.

2. **Worldwide Inventory Chains:** The rise of worldwide stock chains took into account the effective creation and dissemination of products across borders. Organizations

obtained materials and work from various nations, expanding proficiency and bringing down costs.

3. **Monetary Mix:** Monetary business sectors turned out to be progressively coordinated, with streams of capital intersection borders at remarkable levels. This joining brought the two amazing open doors and dangers, as seen in monetary emergencies like the Asian monetary emergency of 1997 and the worldwide monetary emergency of 2008.

4. **Social Trade:** Social globalization thrived, driven by the worldwide spread of media, diversion, and mainstream society. Hollywood motion pictures, global music, and computerized stages associated individuals around the world.

VII. Globalization's Effect and Difficulties

1. **Monetary Development:** Globalization has added to huge financial development and the decrease of destitution in many areas of the planet.

2. **Pay Imbalance:** Nonetheless, it has likewise been connected to rising pay disparity inside and between nations, which has turned into a hostile issue.

3. **Social Homogenization:** Social globalization has prompted worries about social homogenization and the disintegration of nearby customs and personalities.

4. **Ecological Worries:** Globalization has added to natural difficulties, including environmental change and asset exhaustion.

5. **Political and Social Developments:** Globalization has been joined by political and social developments pushing for social protection, native privileges, and fair exchange rehearses.

VIII. The Continuous Development of Globalization

1. **Computerized Globalization:** The advanced economy, described by web based business, remote work, and the development of on-line administrations, is reshaping worldwide communications.
2. **International Movements:** International shifts, like the ascent of China as a worldwide power and evolving partnerships, are modifying the elements of globalization.
3. **Supportability and Morals:** Manageability concerns and moral contemplations are turning out to be progressively key to conversations about globalization.

2.2 Key Drivers of Globalization

Globalization is a multi-layered and extraordinary peculiarity that has reshaped the world in significant ways. It envelops the rising interconnectedness and relationship of countries and people across the globe. While globalization is a complicated cycle impacted by various variables, a few key drivers play had a focal influence in pushing it forward. This exposition investigates these key drivers, featuring their importance and effect on the worldwide scene.

1. Mechanical Headways

One of the main drivers of globalization is the quick headway of innovation, especially in the domain of data and correspondence innovation (ICT). The accompanying innovative improvements have sped up globalization:

1. **The Web:** The web has reformed the manner in which individuals and organizations associate worldwide. It works with momentary correspondence, data sharing, and admittance to an immense internet based commercial center.
2. **Versatile Innovation:** The expansion of cell phones and cell phones has expanded worldwide network. Versatile innovation

permits people to get to data, direct business, and convey across borders easily.

3. **Advanced Stages:** The ascent of computerized stages, like virtual entertainment, internet business sites, and online commercial centers, has made new roads for worldwide collaboration, exchange, and social trade.

4. **Broadcast communications:** Advances in broadcast communications, including high velocity information transmission and satellite innovation, have empowered worldwide voice and information correspondence, making the world more available.

2. Exchange Progression and Monetary Strategies

1. **International alliances:** Two-sided and multilateral international alliances, like NAFTA (North American International alliance) and the European Association's single market, have brought down exchange hindrances and empowered worldwide trade.

2. **Liberation:** Financial liberation in different areas, including money and broadcast communications, has considered more noteworthy cross-line venture and contest.

3. **Venture Strategies:** Approaches that draw in unfamiliar direct speculation (FDI) and worldwide organizations (MNCs) have cultivated worldwide financial combination.

4. **Monetary Coordination:** The globalization of monetary business sectors has prompted the development of capital across borders, influencing both speculation and monetary strength.

3. Transportation and Foundation

1. **Delivery and Coordinated operations:** The improvement of containerization and proficient delivery techniques has diminished transportation costs and considered the extension of worldwide exchange.

2. **Air Travel:** The development of worldwide air travel has made it more straightforward for individuals to get across borders for business, the travel industry, and instruction.

3. **Street and Rail Organizations:** Further developed street and rail networks have empowered the effective development of products inside and between nations.

4. Global Companies (MNCs)

1. **Worldwide Stockpile Chains:** MNCs have made complex worldwide inventory chains, upgrading creation cycles and decreasing expenses by obtaining materials and parts from various nations.

2. **Unfamiliar Direct Venture (FDI):** MNCs put resources into unfamiliar business sectors, bringing capital, innovation, and work chances to have nations while growing their worldwide reach.

3. **Advancement and Innovation Move:** MNCs frequently act as courses for the exchange of innovation and development across borders.

4. **Market Development:** By working in different nations, MNCs make new business sectors for their items and administrations, adding to expanded worldwide exchange.

5. Political Choices and Peaceful accords

1. **Economic deals:** Respective and multilateral economic deals, like the Transoceanic Organization (TPP) and the Far reaching Monetary and Economic deal (CETA), play had an essential impact in advancing exchange and financial mix.

2. **Speculation Advancement:** Legislatures frequently carry out approaches to draw in unfamiliar venture, offering impetuses to organizations and making good circumstances for worldwide financial movement.

3. **Worldwide Administration:** Worldwide associations like the World Exchange Association (WTO) and the Assembled Countries (UN) give systems to worldwide collaboration and administration, resolving issues going from exchange questions to environmental change.

6. Social Trade and Media

1. **Media Openness:** The worldwide availability of media through TV, film, music, and the web has presented individuals to assorted societies and points of view.
2. **Online Entertainment:** Web-based entertainment stages empower people to interface and offer thoughts and encounters across borders, cultivating worldwide networks and developments.
3. **Mainstream society:** The spread of mainstream society peculiarities, like Hollywood films and worldwide music, has made a common worldwide social jargon.

7. Movement and Diaspora People group

1. **Work Portability:** The development of individuals across borders for work, training, and family reunification has added to social variety and monetary incorporation.
2. **Settlements:** Transient specialists frequently send settlements to their nations of origin, adding to monetary turn of events and neediness decrease.
3. **Diaspora People group:** Diaspora people group keep up with attaches with their nations of beginning, working with exchange, speculation, and social trade.

8. Ecological and Asset Concerns

1. **Worldwide Ecological Arrangements:** Peaceful accords and conventions, for example, the Paris Settlement on environmental change, require worldwide collaboration and coordination.
2. **Asset Extraction:** Globalization has prompted the extraction and exchange of normal assets on a worldwide scale, influencing natural manageability.

9. Worldwide Emergencies and Difficulties

1. **Pandemic Reaction:** The Coronavirus pandemic featured the significance of worldwide joint effort in medical care, immunization appropriation, and emergency the executives.
2. **Security Difficulties:** Transnational security dangers, like illegal intimidation and cyberattacks, require worldwide collaboration and knowledge sharing.

10. Segment Movements

1. **Urbanization:** The development of urban communities has made financial centers and focuses of advancement, drawing in ability and venture.
2. **Maturing Populaces:** Maturing populaces in many created nations drive interest for worldwide administrations, including medical services and retirement choices.

2.3 Globalization Theories and Debates

Globalization is a diverse peculiarity that has molded the world in complex ways. As it has advanced, researchers from different disciplines have created hypotheses and taken part in discussions to all the more likely figure out its elements, effects, and suggestions. This article investigates a portion of the key globalization hypotheses and discussions that have arisen in scholar and public talk.

1. Speculations of Globalization

1. Modernization Hypothesis

Modernization hypothesis, which arose during the twentieth 100 years, places that social orders progress through transformative phases. As they modernize and industrialize, they are supposed to embrace Western qualities, establishments, and

ways of life. Defenders contend that globalization is a characteristic consequence of this cycle, as social orders become more interconnected and comparable in their viewpoint.

Investigates: Pundits contend that modernization hypothesis is excessively Eurocentric and neglects to represent the variety of ways to advancement. They likewise guide out that globalization doesn't be guaranteed to lead toward Westernization and can make assorted social and monetary impacts.

2. Reliance Hypothesis

Reliance hypothesis arose because of the worldwide differences in financial turn of events. It fights that the worldwide monetary framework propagates disparity by leaning toward center (created) nations over fringe (immature) nations. Reliance scholars contend that globalization frequently extends this inconsistent relationship by taking advantage of assets and work in the outskirts.

Scrutinizes: Pundits propose that reliance hypothesis distorts the intricacies of worldwide monetary communications and that its attention on financial abuse may not completely catch the multi-layered nature of globalization.

3. World Frameworks Hypothesis

World frameworks hypothesis, created by Immanuel Wallerstein during the 1970s, expands on reliance hypothesis and sets that the world works as a solitary, interconnected framework with a center, semi-fringe, and outskirts. It accentuates the verifiable and primary factors that shape worldwide financial and political relations.

Scrutinizes: While world frameworks hypothesis offers important experiences into worldwide disparities, a few pundits contend that it distorts the world's intricacy and may not completely represent the job of culture, governmental issues, and organization in forming worldwide elements.

4. **Globalization as a Social Peculiarity**

A few researchers center around the social components of globalization, underscoring the spread of thoughts, values, and social items. Social globalization speculations investigate what globalization means for characters, social trade, and the spread of social components around the world.

Evaluates: Discussions encompassing social globalization frequently rotate around worries of social homogenization or social government, where predominant societies might eclipse or disintegrate nearby societies.

5. **Neoliberalism and Monetary Globalization**

Neoliberalism is a financial and political philosophy that underscores unregulated economy free enterprise, liberation, and restricted government mediation. Defenders contend that neoliberal strategies have been instrumental in advancing financial globalization by decreasing exchange obstructions and empowering market-situated changes.

Scrutinizes: Pundits attest that neoliberalism can worsen financial disparities, exploit work and assets, and focus on benefit over friendly government assistance and ecological manageability.

II. Banters on Globalization

1. **Globalization's Effect on Imbalance**

One of the focal discussions encompassing globalization concerns its effect on pay and abundance imbalance. A contend that globalization has prompted more noteworthy worldwide pay imbalance, as abundance becomes packed in center nations and among worldwide organizations. Others battle that globalization has lifted millions out of destitution in emerging nations.

2. **Social Homogenization versus Social Variety**

   The social elements of globalization have led to banters about social homogenization versus social variety. Pundits stress that globalization prompts the spread of Western culture to the detriment of nearby customs. Advocates contend that globalization cultivates social variety by advancing diverse communications and hybridization.

3. **Monetary Mix and Power**

   The discussion over financial globalization spins around the pressure between monetary combination and public sway. Pundits contend that globalization disintegrates public power as worldwide organizations and arrangements impact homegrown approaches. Defenders underscore the advantages of financial combination, like expanded exchange and venture potential open doors.

4. **Globalization's Effect on Work**

   Globalization's impacts on work markets are a subject of continuous discussion. Some contend that globalization prompts the re-appropriating of occupations to nations with lower work costs, adding to work uprooting in center nations. Others battle that globalization can set out new work open doors and advance financial development.

5. **Ecological Manageability**

   Globalization's effect on the climate is a petulant issue. Pundits contend that globalization speeds up natural debasement by empowering asset extraction and fossil fuel byproducts. Defenders recommend that globalization can likewise work with the exchange of green innovations and economical practices.

6. **Globalization and Political Developments**

Globalization has ignited political developments and libertarian reaction in different areas of the planet. Discusses focus on whether globalization sabotages majority rule administration and social union or on the other hand on the off chance that it advances political pluralism and worldwide collaboration.

III. The Fate of Globalization

As globalization keeps on advancing, the discussions and hypotheses encompassing it will probably develop also. Arising patterns, for example, the advanced economy, environmental change, and worldwide wellbeing emergencies, will shape the fate of globalization and bring up new issues and difficulties.

2.4 Contemporary Globalization Trends

Globalization, as a dynamic and steadily developing cycle, keeps on molding the world in significant ways. In the contemporary period, a few key patterns are molding and characterizing the ongoing scene of globalization. These patterns are an impression of the continuous interconnectivity of economies, societies, social orders, and innovations across borders. This paper investigates a portion of the noticeable contemporary globalization drifts that are impacting our present reality.

1. Advanced Globalization

Perhaps of the most extraordinary pattern in contemporary globalization is the ascent of the computerized economy. The expansion of data and correspondence innovation (ICT) and the web have reformed the manner in which individuals and organizations connect around the world. Key parts of advanced globalization include:

1. **Internet business:** The development of online retail and online business stages has made a worldwide commercial center where buyers can get to items and administrations from around the world easily.

2. **Remote Work:** Advances in computerized innovation have worked with remote work courses of action, permitting people to team up on projects and add to associations no matter what their geographic area.

3. **Worldwide Computerized Stages:** Tech monsters like Amazon, Google, Facebook, and Alibaba have become worldwide computerized stages that interface individuals, organizations, and data for a huge scope.

4. **Admittance to Data:** The web gives admittance to a tremendous measure of data, permitting people and associations to remain educated and associated worldwide.

5. **Computerized Installments:** Advanced installment frameworks and cryptographic forms of money are changing worldwide monetary exchanges and cross-line installments.

2. Transnational Partnerships and Supply Chains

1. **Worldwide Stock Chains:** MNCs have laid out complex worldwide inventory chains, advancing creation processes and obtaining materials and parts from various nations.

2. **Offshoring and Re-appropriating:** Organizations frequently seaward or re-appropriate specific capabilities or creation cycles to nations with cost benefits.

3. **MNCs in Developing Business sectors:** Organizations from developing business sectors, like China and India, are becoming key part in the worldwide economy, testing the predominance of conventional Western MNCs.

4. **Corporate Social Obligation:** There is a developing accentuation on corporate social obligation (CSR) in light of worries about work conditions, ecological supportability, and moral strategic policies in worldwide stock chains.

3. Ecological Manageability

The issue of ecological manageability has acquired noticeable quality in contemporary globalization conversations. Globalization has both positive and negative natural effects, prompting patterns, for example,

1. **Feasible Stock Chains:** Organizations are progressively taking on maintainable practices in their stockpile chains, zeroing in on decreasing fossil fuel byproducts, preserving assets, and limiting waste.
2. **Peaceful accords:** Peaceful accords, for example, the Paris Settlement on environmental change, reflect worldwide endeavors to by and large address ecological difficulties.
3. **Green Innovations:** The globalization of information and innovation move is working with the spread of green advances and feasible arrangements across borders.
4. **Shopper Mindfulness:** Buyers are turning out to be more aware of the natural impression of items and are requesting supportable and eco-accommodating choices.

4. Social Hybridization and Worldwide Personalities

1. **Social Hybridization:** The trading of thoughts, values, and social components from various areas of the planet has prompted social hybridization, where societies mix and make novel blends.
2. **Worldwide Mainstream society:** Mainstream society peculiarities, for example, K-pop and worldwide blockbuster films, have acquired worldwide followings, testing the predominance of Western mainstream society.
3. **Social Conservation:** Close by hybridization, there is a developing accentuation on protecting and rejuvenating neighborhood societies despite globalization.

5. International Moves and Economic alliance

1. **Ascent of China:** China's rise as a worldwide monetary force to be reckoned with has moved the harmony between financial power and exchange connections.
2. **Economic deals:** Reciprocal and local economic deals, like the Thorough and Moderate Arrangement for Transoceanic Association (CPTPP), are molding exchange examples and globalization.
3. **Regionalism:** Territorial monetary coalitions, similar to the European Association and the African Association, assume a huge part in forming local and worldwide exchange.

6. Worldwide Wellbeing and Pandemics

1. **Travel Limitations:** Travel limitations and disturbances to worldwide stockpile chains have uncovered weaknesses in the interconnected worldwide economy.
2. **Immunization Appropriation:** The conveyance of antibodies and admittance to medical care assets have become worldwide issues requiring global participation.
3. **Advanced Wellbeing:** The pandemic has sped up the reception of computerized wellbeing advances, encouraging worldwide joint effort in medical care development.

7. Movement and Diaspora People group

1. **Work Portability:** Talented and incompetent work relocation stays a vital component of contemporary globalization, adding to financial turn of events and social variety.
2. **Settlements:** Transient laborers frequently send settlements to their nations of origin, giving an essential kind of revenue and supporting monetary turn of events.
3. **Worldwide Diaspora Organizations:** Diaspora people group keep up major areas of strength for with their nations of beginning, working with exchange, speculation, and social trade.

8. Worldwide Administration and Global Organizations

1. **Worldwide Collaboration:** Tending to worldwide difficulties, for example, environmental change, requires global participation and multilateral methodologies.
2. **Change Endeavors:** Discussions go on about the viability and change of global associations like the Unified Countries and the World Exchange Association.
3. **Non-State Entertainers:** Non-legislative associations (NGOs), common society gatherings, and transnational support networks assume persuasive parts in molding worldwide administration plans.

3

Chapter3

Sashetization: Concept And Context

The idea of "Sashetization" is a moderately new term that has arisen in the talk encompassing globalization, culture, and personality. While it may not be all around as generally perceived as globalization itself, Sashetization is acquiring consideration as a significant peculiarity deeply shaping contemporary social orders. In this article, we will dig into the idea of Sashetization, investigating its starting points, key attributes, suggestions, and difficulties.

1. Grasping Sashetization
1.1 Meaning of Sashetization
The expression "Sashetization" is gotten from "sashay," and that means to move with a certain and relaxed style. Sashetization can be characterized as the interaction through which people and networks specifically embrace, adjust, or hybridize components of worldwide culture while keeping an unmistakable and certain nearby personality. It addresses a nuanced reaction to globalization, where people and gatherings draw in with worldwide impacts without fundamentally acclimatizing into a homogenized worldwide culture.

1.2 Beginnings of Sashetization

Sashetization is an idea that has developed because of the difficulties presented by globalization, especially in the domain of culture and personality. It is established in the acknowledgment that globalization, with its unavoidable social impacts and interconnectedness, doesn't be guaranteed to prompt the disintegration of nearby characters. All things being equal, Sashetization recognizes that people and networks can draw in with worldwide culture according to their own preferences, specifically taking on angles that impact them while saving their exceptional social legacy.

2. Key Qualities of Sashetization

2.1 Particular Commitment

A focal quality of Sashetization is the specific commitment with worldwide culture. Instead of latently tolerating or dismissing worldwide impacts, people and networks effectively pick which components to embrace and how to integrate them into their lives. This specific methodology takes into consideration a feeling of organization and command over social character.

2.2 Protection of Nearby Personality

Sashetization underlines the safeguarding of nearby personality. While drawing in with worldwide culture, people and networks find purposeful ways to protect their exceptional practices, customs, dialects, and values. This safeguarding is a key part of Sashetization, guaranteeing that neighborhood personalities stay dynamic and important despite globalization.

2.3 Social Hybridization

Sashetization frequently includes a course of social hybridization. This implies that people and networks mix worldwide and nearby components to make a particular social combination. Social hybridization can appear in different ways, like in craftsmanship, style, cooking, and language. It mirrors the imaginative and dynamic nature of Sashetization.

2.4 Certainty and Organization

Sashetization is portrayed by certainty and organization. Those participated in Sashetization are not uninvolved beneficiaries of worldwide culture but rather dynamic members who pursue purposeful decisions about which worldwide impacts to integrate into their lives. This feeling of organization engages people and networks to shape their social personality in a globalized world.

3. Ramifications of Sashetization

3.1 Social Variety

Sashetization adds to the conservation and festivity of social variety. By taking into account the concurrence of worldwide and nearby components, Sashetization enhances the social woven artwork of social orders. It cultivates a climate where different practices and customs can flourish one next to the other, advancing diverse comprehension and appreciation.

3.2 Social Strength

Sashetization upgrades social strength. Notwithstanding globalization's homogenizing inclinations, Sashetization enables networks to adjust and develop while holding their social roots. This flexibility assists networks with exploring the difficulties of an influencing world while keeping a feeling of character and progression.

3.3 Worldwide Exchange

Sashetization advances worldwide discourse and trade. It urges people and networks to draw in with others from various social foundations, encouraging diverse communications and shared learning. This exchange adds to a more interconnected and socially rich worldwide society.

3.4 Individual Personality

On an individual level, Sashetization permits people to build their personalities in a manner that mirrors their extraordinary encounters and inclinations. It offers a structure for people to explore the intricacies of present day character, where worldwide and nearby impacts meet.

4. Difficulties of Sashetization

4.1 Social Apportionment

One test is the gamble of social apportionment, where components of a minimized or minority culture are taken on by a prevailing society without legitimate affirmation or regard. Sashetization ought to be aware of staying away from social appointment and guaranteeing that social trades are led morally and deferentially.

4.2 Social Weakening

Now and again, the course of Sashetization might prompt social weakening, where the uniqueness of neighborhood customs and customs is compromised. Finding some kind of harmony between embracing worldwide impacts and protecting nearby character requires cautious thought.

4.3 Outer Tensions

Outside pressures, for example, financial powers and media impact, can affect the decisions in their Sashetization cycle. These tensions may in some cases lead to the careless reception of worldwide patterns or the disintegration of nearby customs.

4.4 Character Disarray

Sashetization can likewise bring about character disarray for people exploring different social impacts. This can prompt inquiries of validness and having a place, expecting people to wrestle with complex personality issues.

5. Instances of Sashetization

5.1 Food

Numerous contemporary foods all over the planet show Sashetization. Gourmet experts and food aficionados frequently integrate worldwide fixings and cooking methods into conventional dishes, making special and invigorating culinary encounters.

5.2 Design

Design is a domain where Sashetization is promptly clear. Planners and design devotees draw motivation from assorted worldwide sources, mixing customary and contemporary styles to make particular design articulations.

5.3 Music

Music kinds frequently go through Sashetization. Performers combine conventional and present day melodic components, bringing about imaginative and internationally engaging music. Types like world combination and combination jazz epitomize this pattern.

5.4 Language and Correspondence

In the domain of language and correspondence, people might embrace components of worldwide dialects, like English, while keeping up with their local dialects. This semantic hybridization mirrors the standards of Sashetization.

3.1 Defining Sashetization

In an undeniably interconnected and globalized world, the expression "Sashetization" has arisen as an idea that catches an exceptional way to deal with drawing in with worldwide culture while protecting neighborhood characters and customs. This exposition looks to give a far reaching meaning of Sashetization, investigating its starting points, center standards, and suggestions. Sashetization addresses a nuanced reaction to the difficulties presented by globalization, stressing specific commitment, social trustworthiness, and a sure hug of both worldwide and neighborhood impacts.

1. The Beginning of Sashetization
1.1. A Lively Beginning

The expression "Sashetization" draws its lively motivation from "sashay," which means a sure and trendy way of strolling. This decision of phrasing highlights that Sashetization is definitely not a uninvolved reaction to globalization yet a functioning and confident commitment with it. It recommends a purposeful and elegant way to deal with exploring the intricacies of a globalized world.

1.2. A Reaction to Globalization

Sashetization has arisen as a reaction to the difficulties and open doors introduced by globalization. As the world turns out to be more interconnected, societies, customs, and personalities are progressively impacted by worldwide powers. Sashetization recognizes this reality yet proposes a method for drawing in with worldwide culture while safeguarding the uprightness and uniqueness of neighborhood characters.

2. Characterizing Sashetization

2.1. Specific Commitment

At its center, Sashetization includes specific commitment with worldwide culture. As opposed to latently tolerating or dismissing worldwide impacts, people and networks settle on cognizant decisions about which components to embrace and how to integrate them into their lives. This specific methodology is a sign of Sashetization, considering a feeling of organization and command over social personality.

2.2. Social Uprightness

Protection of social trustworthiness is an essential part of Sashetization. It underlines the significance of defending nearby practices, customs, dialects, and values even as people and networks draw in with worldwide culture. Social uprightness guarantees that nearby personalities stay energetic and significant even with globalization.

2.3. Innovative Hybridization

Sashetization frequently includes an innovative flow of social hybridization. This implies that people and networks mix worldwide and nearby components to make an unmistakable social combination. Social hybridization can appear in different parts of life, including craftsmanship, style, food, and language. It mirrors the dynamic and advancing nature of Sashetization.

2.4. Certainty and Office

Sashetization is described by certainty and office. Those participated in Sashetization are not latent beneficiaries of worldwide culture but rather dynamic members who settle on conscious decisions about which worldwide impacts to integrate into their lives. This feeling of organization engages people and networks to shape their social personality in a globalized world.

3. Key Standards of Sashetization

3.1. The Guideline of Congruity

Sashetization looks to work out some kind of harmony among worldwide and neighborhood impacts. It perceives that people and networks can embrace worldwide culture without compromising the respectability of their neighborhood character. This standard features that social conjunction isn't just imaginable yet additionally improving.

3.2. The Standard of Variation

Variation is a critical rule of Sashetization. It recognizes that societies are not static however advance over the long run. Sashetization urges transformation to changing worldwide elements while residual established in social customs. It considers the fuse of novel thoughts and practices in a manner that reverberates with neighborhood values.

3.3. The Rule of Certainty

Certainty is key to Sashetization. It underscores the significance of being confident in one's social character while drawing in with worldwide impacts. Sashetization urges people and networks to move toward globalization with certainty, realizing that their remarkable character is a wellspring of solidarity.

3.4. The Standard of Inclusivity

Sashetization elevates inclusivity and receptiveness to assorted social impacts. It urges people and networks to gain from and draw in with individuals from various foundations. Inclusivity is viewed as a method for improving one's own social collection while encouraging multifaceted comprehension.

4. Ramifications of Sashetization

4.1. Social Variety

One of the huge ramifications of Sashetization is the advancement of social variety. By taking into consideration the concurrence of worldwide and neighborhood components,

Sashetization enhances the social embroidered artwork of social orders. It encourages a climate where different practices and customs can flourish next to each other, advancing diverse comprehension and appreciation.

4.2. Social Strength

Sashetization upgrades social flexibility. Notwithstanding globalization's homogenizing propensities, Sashetization enables networks to adjust and advance while holding their social roots. This flexibility assists networks with exploring the difficulties of an impacting world while keeping a feeling of personality and progression.

4.3. Worldwide Discourse

Sashetization advances worldwide discourse and trade. It urges people and networks to draw in with others from various social foundations, cultivating multifaceted connections and shared learning. This exchange adds to a more interconnected and socially rich worldwide society.

4.4. Individual Character

On an individual level, Sashetization permits people to develop their characters in a manner that mirrors their novel encounters and inclinations. It offers a structure for people to explore the intricacies of current personality, where worldwide and neighborhood impacts converge.

3.2 Origins and Emergence

The idea of Sashetization, portrayed by its one of a kind way to deal with exploring globalization while safeguarding nearby social personalities, has earned expanding respect and importance in contemporary conversations. To comprehend Sashetization completely, investigating its starting points and emergence is fundamental. This exposition dives into the verifiable and cultural elements that added to the improvement of Sashetization as a reaction to the difficulties and open doors presented by globalization.

1. **Verifiable Setting**

   1.1. The Globalization Peculiarity

   Sashetization arises with regards to globalization, a multi-layered peculiarity that has been developing for a really long time. The foundations of globalization can be followed back to early mankind's set of experiences, with the trading of products, thoughts, and

   societies across old shipping lanes like the Silk Street. Nonetheless, the speed and size of globalization sped up altogether in the cutting edge time.

   1.2. Early Globalization Waves

   The Period of Investigation in the fifteenth and sixteenth hundreds of years denoted a urgent stage in globalization, as European wayfarers set out on journeys that extended the well explored parts of the planet and laid out associations between recently disengaged districts. This period saw the trading of products, like flavors and valuable metals, between the Old World (Europe, Asia, and Africa) and the New World (the Americas).

   1.3. Industrialization and Innovative Advances

   The Modern Unrest in the eighteenth and nineteenth hundreds of years moved globalization further. Headways in transportation, like the steam motor and railroads, worked with the development of individuals and products across borders. Besides, the message and later correspondence advances associated far off districts, making data trade more fast.

2. **Rise of Sashetization**

   2.1. Early Responses to Globalization

As globalization extended, social orders wrestled with its suggestions. The underlying reactions frequently elaborate obstruction, variation, or osmosis. A few networks opposed the infringement of unfamiliar impacts, trying to safeguard their customary lifestyles. Others adjusted to worldwide changes by incorporating unfamiliar components into their societies. Absorption, then again, involved the total reception of unfamiliar qualities and practices, frequently to the detriment of neighborhood characters.

2.2. The Constraints of Osmosis

After some time, the restrictions of absorption became apparent. While globalization brought new open doors and thoughts, it additionally took steps to disintegrate exceptional social characters. The craving to protect social genuineness and uniqueness turned into a developing worry for networks around the world.

2.3. The Introduction of Sashetization

Sashetization arose as a reaction to these difficulties. It addresses a cognizant work to draw in with worldwide culture while keeping up with the honesty of nearby characters. The actual term, got from "sashay," conveys a feeling of certain and purposeful commitment with worldwide impacts. Instead of tolerating globalization as a widely inclusive power, Sashetization offers an elective methodology, one that consolidates selectivity, social honesty, and imagination.

3. Center Standards of Sashetization

3.1. Specific Commitment

At the core of Sashetization is the guideline of specific commitment. It accentuates the organization of people and networks in picking which parts of worldwide culture to embrace. This selectivity takes into consideration a customized and intentional way to deal with globalization.

3.2. Social Honesty

Sashetization puts a high worth on social honesty. It empowers the conservation of neighborhood customs, dialects, customs, and values, guaranteeing that they stay energetic and pertinent even with globalization's persuasions.

3.3. Imaginative Hybridization

Sashetization frequently includes imaginative hybridization. This interaction permits people and networks to mix worldwide and nearby components to make interesting social combinations. It praises the dynamic and developing nature of culture.

3.4. Certainty and Office

Sashetization is portrayed by certainty and office. It enables people and networks to draw in with worldwide culture with trust in their own personality. This feeling of organization empowers them to effectively shape their social accounts.

4. Cultural Elements Adding to Sashetization

4.1. Social Safeguarding Developments

Sashetization has been impacted by social protection developments that arose because of the apparent dangers presented by globalization. These developments tried to protect customary practices, dialects, and customs, making way for a more purposeful way to deal with social commitment.

4.2. Mechanical Headways

Mechanical progressions play had a crucial impact in the development of Sashetization. The advanced age has permitted people and networks to get to worldwide data and associate with assorted societies while keeping up with neighborhood ties. The web, specifically, has given a stage to innovative articulation and social trade.

4.3. Multifaceted Discourse

Multifaceted discourse, worked with by globalization itself, has added to the improvement of Sashetization. As individuals from various foundations collaborate and share their encounters, they figure out how to see the value in the benefit of saving social variety while drawing in with worldwide impacts.

5. Ramifications of Sashetization

5.1. Social Variety

Sashetization advances and celebrates social variety. By considering the concurrence of worldwide and neighborhood components, it advances the social embroidered artwork of social orders. This variety encourages culturally diverse comprehension and appreciation.

5.2. Social Flexibility

Sashetization improves social flexibility. It engages networks to adjust and advance while holding their social roots. This versatility assists networks with exploring the difficulties of an impacting world while keeping a feeling of personality and congruity.

5.3. Individual Strengthening

On an individual level, Sashetization engages people to develop their personalities in a manner that mirrors their novel encounters and inclinations. It gives a system to exploring the intricacies of present day personality, where worldwide and nearby impacts converge.

3.3Cultural and Social Implications

Sashetization, described by its certain and specific commitment with worldwide culture while protecting neighborhood characters, has critical social and social ramifications. This way to deal with exploring globalization recognizes the interconnectedness of the world yet underscores the significance of keeping up with social validness and variety. In this article, we investigate the social and social ramifications of Sashetization, remembering its effect for social variety, social conservation, diverse comprehension, and individual personality.

1. Observing Social Variety

1.1. Social Pluralism

Sashetization celebrates social pluralism by taking into account the concurrence of worldwide and nearby components. It advances that different societies and customs can flourish next to each other in an interconnected world. As people and networks draw in with worldwide culture while safeguarding their nearby characters, they add to the woven artwork of social variety.

1.2. Multifaceted Amalgamation

Sashetization frequently includes imaginative hybridization, where worldwide and nearby components mix to make interesting social unions. This amalgamation features the unique idea of culture and the potential for advancement when different social impacts converge. It encourages a climate where customary and contemporary components can exist together amicably.

2. Social Safeguarding

2.1. Protecting Social Legacy

One of the crucial social ramifications of Sashetization is its accentuation on social safeguarding. It urges networks to protect their social legacy, including dialects, customs, ceremonies, and creative articulations. Social safeguarding developments frequently line up with the standards of Sashetization, endeavoring to guarantee that nearby customs stay energetic and significant despite globalization.

2.2. Renewing Customs

Sashetization gives a structure to endlessly renewing customs. By drawing in with worldwide culture in their own specific manner, networks can track down better approaches to mix their practices with imperativeness and importance. This renewal frequently includes imaginative reevaluation and variation of social practices.

3. Diverse Comprehension

3.1. Encouraging Compassion

Sashetization cultivates culturally diverse comprehension by empowering people and networks to draw in with worldwide societies consciously and straightforwardly. This commitment advances sympathy and appreciation for the encounters and points of view of others. It destroys generalizations and biases, encouraging a more comprehensive and lenient society.

3.2. Connecting Social Partitions

Sashetization fills in as an extension between societies. It empowers people to investigate and gain from various social customs without essentially forsaking their own. This scaffold building adds to the separating of social obstructions and advances serene conjunction in an undeniably interconnected world.

4. Individual Personality

4.1. Individual Strengthening

Sashetization enables people to build their personalities in a manner that mirrors their remarkable encounters and inclinations. It offers a structure for exploring the intricacies of current character, where worldwide and neighborhood impacts cross. This individual strengthening permits people to embrace their social legacy certainly while investigating new social skylines.

4.2. Diverse Characters

In a world described by globalization, people frequently have multi-layered characters that draw from different social sources. Sashetization recognizes and embraces this intricacy, permitting people to have liquid and developing characters that incorporate both worldwide and nearby perspectives.

5. Difficulties and Contemplations

5.1. Social Apportionment

One test related with Sashetization is the gamble of social apportionment. The particular reception of components from one more culture ought to be finished with deference and awareness, recognizing the social starting points and meaning of those components. Keeping away from social harshness or abuse chasing Sashetization is fundamental.

5.2. Adjusting Conservation and Development

One more thought is finding some kind of harmony between social conservation and development. While Sashetization empowers the conservation of social legacy, it additionally embraces inventive hybridization and variation. Networks should explore this equilibrium to guarantee that their customs stay pertinent while regarding their social genuineness.

3.4 Economic and Technological Aspects

Sashetization, with its accentuation on certain and particular commitment with worldwide culture while saving nearby characters, has huge monetary and innovative ramifications. As the world turns out to be progressively interconnected, monetary and mechanical elements assume a vital part in forming the elements of Sashetization. This article investigates the financial and mechanical parts of Sashetization, remembering its effect for monetary turn of events, advanced innovation, business, and development.

1. **Financial Turn of events**
   1.1. Neighborhood Financial Versatility

Sashetization can add to neighborhood financial versatility. By protecting and celebrating nearby social customs, networks can use their interesting way of life as a wellspring of financial strength. This can prompt the improvement of social the travel industry, distinctive items, and other specialty showcases that take care of both nearby and worldwide crowds.

1.2. Social Businesses

Sashetization frequently advances the development of social ventures. These ventures incorporate many areas, including expressions, creates, music, design, and cooking. They blossom with the novel social articulations that Sashetization empowers. Social enterprises add to monetary advancement as well as act as vehicles for social conservation and advancement.

2. **Advanced Innovation**
   2.1. Admittance to Worldwide Business sectors

Advanced innovation has empowered people and networks participated in Sashetization to get to worldwide business sectors easily. Online stages, internet business, and web-based entertainment give roads to displaying and offering nearby items and social encounters to a worldwide crowd. This advanced presence takes into account financial open doors that were once out of reach.

2.2. Social Trade

The web and advanced innovation work with social trade and diverse discourse. People and networks can interface with individuals from various areas of the planet, sharing their social practices and items carefully. This trade encourages a more profound comprehension of different societies and can prompt financial coordinated efforts and organizations.

3. Business

3.1. Social Business

Sashetization frequently encourages social business venture, where people or gatherings foster inventive undertakings revolved around their social legacy. These endeavors might incorporate comprehensive developments, distinctive items, culinary encounters, and the sky is the limit from there. Social business visionaries influence their novel social personality to make attractive items and administrations.

3.2. Social Business

Social business is one more aspect of Sashetization. A few people and associations utilize their social drives for financial increase as well as to address social and ecological difficulties. This approach lines up with the standards of Sashetization by stressing social obligation and local area improvement.

4. Development

4.1. Innovative Hybridization

Sashetization energizes imaginative hybridization, where worldwide and nearby components converge to make creative arrangements and items. This course of mixing social practices and contemporary impacts can prompt novel developments in different fields, including workmanship, plan, innovation, and the sky is the limit from there.

4.2. Social Development Center points

Certain areas or networks took part in Sashetization might become centers for social advancement. These center points draw in imaginative people and business visionaries keen on investigating the convergence of culture and innovation. Such development communities can drive monetary development while safeguarding and celebrating social variety.

5. Difficulties and Contemplations

5.1. Computerized Separation

A critical test connected with the mechanical parts of Sashetization is the computerized partition. Not all networks have equivalent admittance to computerized innovation and the web. This gap can set out abberations in monetary open doors and obstruct the capacity of certain networks to connect really in Sashetization.

5.2. Protected innovation

The security of protected innovation freedoms is a thought in the monetary parts of Sashetization. As social articulations are displayed and promoted worldwide, guaranteeing that nearby makers and networks benefit from their social advancements becomes fundamental. Resolving issues of licensed innovation and fair pay is pivotal for supporting social business venture.

4

Chapter4

Globalization's Impact on Sashetization

Globalization and Sashetization address two interconnected peculiarities that significantly affect the manner in which people and networks draw in with culture and personality in an undeniably interconnected world. While globalization has the ability to homogenize societies and advance a worldwide monoculture, Sashetization gives a counter-story, underscoring specific commitment with worldwide impacts while protecting neighborhood personalities. This article dives into the mind boggling connection among globalization and Sashetization, investigating how globalization has molded the rise and development of Sashetization and its suggestions for culture, character, and society.

1. **The Globalization Worldview**
1.1. Globalization Characterized
Globalization is a diverse cycle described by the rising interconnectedness of economies, societies, and social orders on a worldwide scale. It includes the progression of merchandise, administrations, data, thoughts, and individuals across borders. Mechanical progressions, like the web and media communications, have sped up the speed of globalization, making the world

more interconnected than any other time.

1.2. Globalization's Social Effect

One of the focal parts of globalization is its social effect. It has worked with the worldwide scattering of social items, thoughts, and practices. While this has set out open doors for diverse trade and understanding, it has likewise prompted worries about social homogenization and the disintegration of neighborhood personalities.

2. Sashetization: A Reaction to Globalization

2.1. The Rise of Sashetization

Sashetization arose as a reaction to the difficulties presented by globalization's social effect. It addresses a cognizant work to draw in with worldwide culture while safeguarding neighborhood personalities. The expression "Sashetization," got from "sashay," conveys a feeling of sure and purposeful commitment with worldwide impacts. It offers a nuanced option in contrast to the latent acknowledgment or discount dismissal of worldwide culture.

2.2. Key Standards of Sashetization

Particular Commitment: At the center of Sashetization is the rule of specific commitment. People and networks pick which components of worldwide culture to embrace, taking into account organization and command over social character.

Social Trustworthiness: Sashetization stresses the safeguarding of nearby social honesty. It energizes the protecting of conventional practices, dialects, customs, and values, guaranteeing they stay dynamic and pertinent.

Imaginative Hybridization: Sashetization frequently includes innovative hybridization, where worldwide and neighborhood components mix to make particular social combinations. This cycle mirrors the unique idea of culture.

Certainty and Organization: Sashetization enables people and networks to draw in with worldwide culture with trust in their own personality, effectively forming their social accounts.

3. Globalization's Effect on Sashetization
3.1. Social Streams

Globalization has worked with the progression of social items, thoughts, and practices across borders. This social trade has given the unrefined substance to Sashetization. People and networks can draw from a tremendous worldwide social collection, choosing components that resound with their neighborhood character.

3.2. Mechanical Empowering influences

Mechanical headways, like the web and virtual entertainment, play had a urgent impact in Sashetization. These stages empower people and networks to promptly get to and draw in with worldwide culture more. The computerized age has democratized social articulation, permitting assorted voices to be heard.

3.3. Financial Open doors

Globalization has set out financial open doors that can uphold Sashetization endeavors. The worldwide market for social items and encounters has extended, giving a stage to people and networks participated in Sashetization to feature and adapt their social contributions.

3.4. Social Mindfulness and Training

Globalization has increased social mindfulness and schooling. People are presented to a more extensive exhibit of social viewpoints, encouraging a more noteworthy appreciation for social variety. This mindfulness can fuel the craving to participate in Sashetization for the purpose of protecting and commending one's own way of life.

4. Suggestions for Culture and Personality
4.1. Social Variety

Globalization and Sashetization cross in their effect on social variety. While globalization can possibly homogenize societies, Sashetization celebrates and saves social variety. It takes into account the concurrence of worldwide and neighborhood components, improving the social embroidered artwork of social orders.

4.2. Social Conservation and Advancement

Sashetization advances both social protection and development. It energizes the shielding of conventional practices while considering their innovative reevaluation and transformation. This harmony among protection and advancement is fundamental for the essentialness of societies.

4.3. Personality Arrangement

Globalization and Sashetization impact the arrangement of individual and aggregate characters. Globalization opens people to different social impacts, taking into account the development of diverse personalities. Sashetization enables people to shape their characters with certainty, embracing both worldwide and nearby viewpoints.

5. Difficulties and Pressures

5.1. Social Allocation

One of the difficulties in the connection among globalization and Sashetization is the gamble of social allocation. Globalization can some of the time lead to the careless reception of components from different societies, bringing up issues of realness and regard. Sashetization tries to draw in with worldwide culture consciously and carefully.

5.2. Financial Differences

Globalization can worsen financial variations, which might influence the capacity of networks to take part in Sashetization. Financial requirements can restrict admittance to assets and open doors for social protection and advancement.

6. Future Headings

The connection among globalization and Sashetization is dynamic and advancing. As globalization keeps on molding the world, Sashetization offers a structure for people and networks to explore these progressions with certainty while saving their social personalities. Future headings might include:

Moral Globalization: A development towards more moral and capable globalization that regards social variety and supports drives like Sashetization.

Advanced Strengthening: Utilizing computerized innovation to enable minimized networks to all around the world take part in Sashetization and offer their social accounts.

Interconnected Social Organizations: The development of interconnected social organizations that rise above topographical limits, advancing culturally diverse comprehension and cooperation.

4.1 Cultural Homogenization vs. Diversification

The continuous course of globalization has led to a significant social discussion: the strain between social homogenization and expansion. On one hand, globalization can possibly homogenize societies, eradicating nearby customs and characters for a worldwide monoculture. Then again, it can cultivate social expansion by working with culturally diverse trade and saving nearby personalities. This paper investigates the elements, suggestions, and meaning of social homogenization and enhancement with regards to globalization.

1. Social Homogenization

1.1. Definition

Social homogenization alludes to the interaction by which different societies become more comparative and combine towards a typical social structure. This union frequently includes the spread of worldwide social standards, values, practices, and buyer items.

1.2. Components of Homogenization

Media and Diversion: Worldwide media combinations, alongside the web, disperse a predominant culture that frequently reflects Western qualities and ways of life. This can prompt the reception of Western social components around the world.

Commercialization: The worldwide market advances industrialism and the reception of worldwide brands and items, adding to the normalization of tastes and inclinations.

Language: English, as a worldwide most widely used language, can work with social homogenization as it turns into the mechanism for correspondence, schooling, and business.

2. **Social Expansion**

2.1. Definition

Social expansion is the most common way of safeguarding and celebrating social variety despite globalization. It involves the upkeep of nearby practices, customs, dialects, and personalities, frequently in light of the homogenizing powers of globalization.

2.2. Systems of Broadening

Social Conservation: People group effectively work to protect their social legacy, shielding customary practices and values.

Social Trade: Globalization empowers multifaceted trade, cultivating common comprehension and enthusiasm for assorted customs.

Particular Commitment: People and networks connect specifically with worldwide culture, coordinating unfamiliar components into their lives while safeguarding their novel character.

3. **The Elements of Social Homogenization**

3.1. Globalization and Westernization

Social homogenization is frequently connected with Westernization. The predominance of Western culture, energized by monetary and political power, has prompted the worldwide spread of Western qualities, customer items, and way of life decisions. Thus, neighborhood societies might take on Western components to the detriment of their own customs.

3.2. Disintegration of Neighborhood Customs

Social homogenization can bring about the disintegration of neighborhood customs. As worldwide social standards come first, conventional practices might lose importance, prompting a decrease in social variety and character.

4. **The Elements of Social Broadening**

   4.1. Social Conservation Developments

   Social broadening is in many cases driven by social safeguarding developments. Networks and people try to secure and resuscitate their social legacy, perceiving the worth of their interesting practices.

   4.2. Culturally diverse Comprehension

   Social enhancement encourages culturally diverse comprehension and appreciation. Networks participate in discourse, sharing their practices and customs. This trade advances the worldwide social embroidery and advances resilience.

5. **Ramifications of Social Homogenization**

   5.1. Loss of Social Variety

   The essential ramifications of social homogenization is the deficiency of social variety. At the point when societies meet toward a typical worldwide culture, extraordinary customs, dialects, and practices might disappear, prompting social impoverishment.

   5.2. Social Dominion

   Social homogenization can sustain social colonialism, where prevailing societies force their qualities and standards on others. This can sabotage nearby independence and self-assurance.

6. **Ramifications of Social Broadening**

   6.1. Social Enhancement

   Social broadening advances worldwide culture by saving and celebrating different customs. It advances a more pluralistic and comprehensive worldwide society.

   6.2. Flexibility and Character

   Social expansion upgrades social strength and personality. Networks that effectively safeguard their practices are better prepared to adjust to changing worldwide elements while holding their social roots.

7. **The Equilibrium and Importance**

7.1. The Requirement for Equilibrium

It is significant to Adjust social homogenization and expansion. While globalization brings open doors for social trade, monetary turn of events, and multifaceted comprehension, it additionally presents dangers to social variety and personality.

7.2. Meaning of Social Character

Social character is a wellspring of pride and having a place for people and networks. It gives a feeling of progression, having a place, and reason. Protecting social personality is fundamental for keeping a different and socially rich world.

4.2 Economic Opportunities and Challenges

Globalization has changed the monetary scene by growing business sectors, encouraging development, and interfacing organizations around the world. While it has set out various monetary open doors, it has likewise delivered difficulties that require insightful route. This article investigates the financial open doors and difficulties related with globalization and features the significance of proactive techniques for tending to them.

1. Monetary Open doors

1.1. Market Development

Globalization gives organizations admittance to bigger and more different business sectors. Organizations can arrive at clients across the globe, taking advantage of beforehand undiscovered customer bases. This extension of business sectors opens up critical development potential.

1.2. Development and Contest

Globalization encourages advancement through expanded contest. Organizations are constrained to enhance to remain cutthroat on a worldwide scale. This drive for advancement prompts the improvement of new items, administrations, and innovations, helping the two organizations and shoppers.

1.3. Admittance to Assets

Globalization permits organizations to productively get to assets more. Whether it's unrefined components, talented work, or concentrated information, organizations can take advantage of worldwide organizations to address their issues, frequently at lower costs.

1.4. Monetary Development

Globalization can drive monetary development at both the public and worldwide levels. Expanded exchange and venture can help a nation's Gross domestic product, prompting worked on expectations for everyday comforts and open positions. At the worldwide level, interconnected economies can prompt aggregate financial development.

2. Monetary Difficulties

2.1. Pay Imbalance

Globalization has been joined by rising pay imbalance. While it can make abundance for some, it can abandon others. Laborers in low-ability ventures might confront work uprooting and wage stagnation, adding to pay differences.

2.2. Work Relocation

The rethinking and mechanization of occupations in a globalized economy can prompt work uprooting in specific areas. Laborers who miss the mark on abilities required for arising businesses might encounter joblessness or underemployment.

2.3. Ecological Effect

Globalization can strain normal assets and intensify natural difficulties. The expanded development of products and individuals adds to higher fossil fuel byproducts and natural corruption. Maintainability concerns are currently an indispensable piece of the worldwide monetary plan.

2.4. Loss of Social Character

As worldwide brands and shopper culture spread, there is a gamble of the deficiency of neighborhood social personality.

Native enterprises and customs might be eclipsed by worldwide homogenization, affecting social variety.

3. **Systems for Expanding Monetary Open doors**

3.1. Instruction and Ability Improvement

Putting resources into training and expertise improvement is vital for people to make the most of monetary open doors in a globalized world. A talented and versatile labor force can contend really in a quickly changing position market.

3.2. Development and Business venture

Empowering development and business venture can open financial potential. Legislatures and organizations ought to establish a climate that upholds new companies, encourages advancement, and empowers little undertakings to increase.

3.3. Economic alliance and Fair Practices

Nations can arrange economic alliance that advance fair contest and safeguard laborers' privileges. These arrangements can work with exchange while guaranteeing that organizations stick to moral and work guidelines.

3.4. Ecological Obligation

Treating ecological obligation in a serious way is fundamental. Supportable strategic policies, sustainable power, and asset productive advancements can moderate the ecological effect of globalization.

4. **Systems for Tending to Financial Difficulties**

4.1. Social Security Nets

States can lay out hearty social security nets to help laborers impacted by work removal. These security nets can incorporate joblessness benefits, work preparing projects, and backing for progressing to new ventures.

4.2. Comprehensive Arrangements

Arrangements that advance inclusivity are fundamental for tending to pay disparity. Moderate tax assessment, abundance rearrangement, and reasonable admittance to instruction and medical services can assist with connecting the pay hole.

4.3. Ecological Guidelines

Rigid ecological guidelines are important to check the negative natural effect of globalization. State run administrations ought to authorize approaches that advance economical practices and consider organizations responsible for their ecological impression.

4.4. Social Protection

Endeavors to protect social personality are pivotal. This can incorporate advancing nearby enterprises, supporting conventional fine arts, and empowering social trade programs.

4.3 Technological Connectivity

Mechanical network, driven by fast progressions in computerized innovation and media communications, has turned into a characterizing element of our globalized world. It holds the possibility to change economies, social orders, and people's lives by working with correspondence, admittance to data, and amazing open doors for advancement. Notwithstanding, it additionally raises worries about the advanced gap, protection, and the moral ramifications of an undeniably interconnected world. This exposition investigates the idea of mechanical network, its effect, challenges, and the basic of connecting the advanced separation.

1. **Innovative Network Characterized**
   ### 1.1. What Is Innovative Network?
   Innovative availability alludes to the capacity of people, networks, and gadgets to associate and interface flawlessly through computerized implies. It envelops different perspectives:
   Web Access: Admittance to the web and broadband network is a crucial part of innovative network. It empowers correspondence, data access, and cooperation in the computerized economy.
   Interconnected Gadgets: The multiplication of shrewd gadgets, for example, cell phones, tablets, and IoT (Web of Things)

gadgets, adds to network by permitting them to impart and share information.

Correspondence Stages: Informing applications, online entertainment stages, and video conferencing devices work with worldwide correspondence, empowering individuals to interface paying little heed to geological distances.

Distributed computing: Cloud administrations empower information capacity, joint effort, and admittance to assets from anyplace with a web association, advancing network.

1.2. The Job of Mechanical Availability in Globalization

Mechanical network is firmly interwoven with globalization. It supports the fast progression of data, the worldwide development of labor and products, and the interconnectedness of organizations, societies, and social orders. It has sped up globalization by working with cross-line coordinated effort, exchange, and the trading of thoughts.

2. Effect of Mechanical Availability

2.1. Financial Effect

Online business: It empowers web based shopping, growing business sectors and business amazing open doors past topographical limits.

Remote Work: The capacity to work remotely is worked with by computerized network, making it feasible for organizations to take advantage of a worldwide ability pool.

Advanced Development: Network powers development by giving admittance to data, research, and cooperative stages for business visionaries and specialists.

2.2. Social and Social Effect

Worldwide Correspondence: Individuals can associate with companions, family, and partners across the world, encouraging worldwide fellowships and social trade.

Data Access: It gives admittance to a huge storehouse of data, advancing information sharing and social mindfulness.

Social Trade: Web-based entertainment and content-sharing stages permit individuals to share and find out about various societies, encouraging multifaceted comprehension.

2.3. Instructive Effect

Web based Learning: It has made instruction available to people overall through web-based courses, computerized assets, and e-learning stages.

Cooperative Learning: Understudies and instructors can team up around the world, sharing information and encounters.

Admittance to Instructive Assets: Innovative availability guarantees admittance to instructive materials, separating obstructions to learning.

3. **Difficulties and Concerns**

3.1. Advanced Separation

One of the essential difficulties is the advanced separation — the hole between the individuals who approach innovation and availability and the people who don't. This separation compounds existing disparities in schooling, financial open doors, and admittance to data.

3.2. Protection and Security

Mechanical network raises worries about protection and security. As more private data is shared on the web, people and associations are helpless against information breaks, cyberattacks, and observation.

3.3. Moral Contemplations

The moral ramifications of network incorporate issues like advanced dependence, online provocation, falsehood, and the effect of web-based entertainment on psychological well-being.

3.4. Ecological Effect

The natural effect of availability incorporates energy utilization, e-squander, and the carbon impression of server farms and advanced gadgets.

4. **Connecting the Advanced Separation**

4.1. Foundation Advancement

To connect the computerized separation, state run administrations and associations should put resources into building advanced foundation, particularly in underserved regions. This incorporates extending broadband access and further developing organization unwavering quality.

4.2. Reasonableness

Reasonableness is pivotal for guaranteeing that network is available to all. Drives, for example, sponsored web plans and reasonable gadgets can assist lower-pay people with crossing over the computerized partition.

4.3. Advanced Education

Advancing computerized education and advanced abilities is fundamental. Instructive projects can engage people with the information and abilities expected to capitalize on mechanical network.

4.4. Local area Drives

Local area based drives can assist with spanning the computerized partition by giving admittance to innovation and network in underserved regions, cultivating neighborhood advanced biological systems.

4.4 Social and Environmental Consequences

Globalization, portrayed by expanded interconnectedness in economies, societies, and social orders, has had significant social and ecological results. While it has achieved financial development, innovative progressions, and social trade, it has additionally created difficulties connected with disparity, social homogenization, ecological debasement, and the double-dealing of normal assets. This paper investigates the perplexing social and ecological results of globalization and the requirement for mindful and feasible ways to deal with address them.

1. Social Results

1.1. Pay Disparity

Globalization has added to rising pay disparity inside and between nations.

Inside Nations: In numerous countries, the advantages of globalization have excessively accumulated to the well off, fueling pay disparity. High-gifted specialists in areas like innovation and back frequently appreciate significant additions, while low-talented laborers might encounter wage stagnation or occupation removal due to rethinking and computerization.

Between Nations: On a worldwide scale, globalization has prompted pay inconsistencies among created and emerging nations. While a few non-industrial countries have encountered financial development and worked on expectations for everyday comforts, others remain minimized in the worldwide economy.

1.2. Social Homogenization

The spread of worldwide culture can dissolve neighborhood customs and social variety.

Western Predominance: Western social standards and values have frequently assumed a prevailing part in forming worldwide culture. This can prompt the disintegration of native societies and customs, adding to social homogenization.

Social Appointment: The globalization of culture can now and again bring about social allotment, where components of one culture are embraced and commodified by another culture, frequently without legitimate affirmation or regard for the social starting points.

2. Ecological Results

2.1. Ecological Debasement

Globalization has sped up ecological debasement through expanded asset utilization and contamination.

Deforestation: The interest for lumber and farming area has driven deforestation, prompting territory misfortune, biodiversity decline, and fossil fuel byproducts.

Contamination: The globalization of assembling has prompted the arrival of poisons and ozone harming substances. Natural guidelines in a single nation might prompt the movement of contaminating enterprises to nations with remiss guidelines, fueling contamination issues.

2.2. Asset Double-dealing

Globalization has expanded the extraction and double-dealing of normal assets, frequently at unreasonable rates.

Mineral Extraction: The interest for minerals, metals, and uncommon earth components utilized in innovation and assembling has prompted asset extraction in ecologically touchy regions.

Overfishing: The worldwide fish exchange has prompted overfishing in numerous districts, exhausting marine environments and undermining fish stocks.

3. Social and Natural Obligation

3.1. Moral Industrialism

Moral industrialism energizes capable customer decisions that think about friendly and natural effects.

Fair Exchange: Fair exchange drives advance impartial exchanging connections, guaranteeing that makers in non-industrial nations get fair pay for their items.

Manageable Items: Buyers progressively look for items with harmless to the ecosystem accreditations, empowering organizations to take on maintainable practices.

3.2. Corporate Social Obligation

Organizations are progressively embracing corporate social obligation (CSR) practices to address social and ecological worries.

Natural Maintainability: Organizations are embracing eco-accommodating works on, lessening waste, and limiting their carbon impression.

Social Drives: CSR programs support schooling, medical care, and social improvement in networks where organizations work.

3.3. Peaceful accords

Peaceful accords and associations assume a part in resolving worldwide natural issues.

Paris Understanding: The Paris Arrangement intends to battle environmental change by setting focuses for diminishing ozone depleting substance emanations. Countries promise to cooperate to restrict an Earth-wide temperature boost.

Biodiversity Protection: Arrangements like the Show on Natural Variety address the conservation of biodiversity and biological systems.

4. **Offsetting Monetary Development with Supportability**

4.1. Supportable Advancement Objectives (SDGs)

The Unified Countries' SDGs give a system to offsetting financial development with social and natural maintainability.

The fact that addresses financial disparity makes no poverty (sdg 1): Killing destitution a focal objective.

Environment Activity (SDG 13): Fighting environmental change while cultivating monetary development is a key test.

Dependable Utilization and Creation (SDG 12): Advancing reasonable utilization designs is significant for ecological maintainability.

4.2. Roundabout Economy

Changing to a round economy, where assets are reused, reused, and reused, can diminish squander and ecological effect.

Diminish, Reuse, Reuse: Empowering people and organizations to limit squander and boost asset productivity is a focal principle of the roundabout economy.

Broadened Maker Obligation (EPR): EPR approaches consider producers answerable for the whole lifecycle of their items, boosting plan for life span and recyclability.

5

Chapter5

Sashetization's Influence on Globalization

Globalization, the peculiarity of expanded interconnectedness and reliance among countries, has been a characterizing element of the cutting edge world. It has changed the manner in which social orders connect, exchange, and convey, forming our economies, societies, and political scenes. Lately, another idea has arisen that meets with globalization in a significant manner - sashetization. This term alludes to the ascent of little, nimble, and exceptionally specific substances that challenge customary power designs and orders. Sashetization's impact on globalization is an intricate interaction that warrants nearer assessment.

Figuring out Sashetization

The expression "sashetization" draws its foundations from the idea of "sashet," a word begat by Parag Khanna in his book "The Subsequent World: Realms and Impact in the New Worldwide Request." A sashet addresses a little, specific, and exceptionally interconnected element that can apply effect on a worldwide scale. These elements can be countries, partnerships, non-administrative associations, or even people. Sashets are described by their capacity to fight at a surprisingly high level, utilizing their nimbleness, innovation, and organizations to contend and team up on a worldwide stage.

Sashetization addresses a shift away from the conventional idea of force being moved in huge, brought together substances. All things considered, power is diffused across an organization of interconnected sashets. This dissemination of force has significant ramifications for globalization, as it adjusts the elements of worldwide legislative issues, financial matters, and culture.

Sashetization's Effect on Worldwide Legislative issues

One of the main effects of sashetization on globalization is in the domain of worldwide legislative issues. Conventional country states have for some time been the essential entertainers in worldwide relations, with their size and military strength deciding their effect on the worldwide stage. Notwithstanding, sashets, whether they are little countries like Singapore or non-state entertainers like psychological oppressor associations, can upset this customary power structure.

Sashets frequently depend on deviated techniques, for example, digital fighting, monetary fighting, or data fighting, to challenge bigger foes. For instance, more modest countries with cutting edge digital capacities can target bigger countries' basic foundation, causing huge disturbances and evening the odds in worldwide struggles. Additionally, non-state entertainers like WikiLeaks have utilized data fighting to uncover the mysteries of strong countries, testing their predominance in worldwide undertakings.

Additionally, sashets are not restricted to geographic limits. They can frame coalitions and organizations across the world, making new power elements in worldwide governmental issues. For example, the BRICS partnership (Brazil, Russia, India, China, and South Africa) addresses a gathering of sashets that have met up to challenge the strength of Western countries in worldwide foundations like the Unified Countries and the Global Financial Asset.

Sashetization's Impact on Worldwide Financial aspects

In the domain of worldwide financial matters, sashetization has disturbed conventional plans of action and exchange designs. Huge worldwide enterprises, when the goliaths of globalization, presently wind up rivaling more modest, nimbler substances that can rapidly adjust to changing economic situations.

One of the most noticeable instances of sashetization in the business world is the ascent of innovation new companies. These organizations frequently start as little, specific endeavors yet can quickly increase and upset whole ventures. Organizations like Uber, Airbnb, and SpaceX have reshaped the transportation and space ventures, testing laid out players and cultivating advancement.

Moreover, sashets assume a critical part in worldwide stockpile chains. They are much of the time had practical experience in specialty areas of creation, and their capacity to rapidly adjust to showcase requests can fundamentally affect worldwide exchange. The Coronavirus pandemic featured the weaknesses of worldwide stock chains, with disturbances in a single region of the planet influencing ventures and economies around the world. Sashets are at the very front of endeavors to make stronger and nimble stockpile chains.

Besides, sashetization has additionally prompted the ascent of miniature multinationals — little organizations that work worldwide through computerized stages and online business. These organizations can arrive at clients and accomplices all over the planet without the requirement for an actual presence in various nations, further obscuring the lines among nearby and worldwide.

Sashetization's Effect on Worldwide Culture

Culture, as well, isn't resistant to the impact of sashetization. In a globalized world, data and thoughts stream across borders at an uncommon speed, and sashets frequently go about as courses for social trade and development.

One of the most apparent signs of sashetization in worldwide culture is through web-based entertainment and online stages. People and forces to be reckoned with can gather worldwide followings, molding patterns and assessments across borders. Stages like Instagram, TikTok, and YouTube have led to another variety of social diplomats who are not partnered with customary media or amusement aggregates.

Sashets likewise assume a part in saving and advancing nearby societies on the worldwide stage. Little, specific social associations and non-legislative elements can use the force of the web to contact worldwide crowds and promoter for social conservation and variety. This considers a more extravagant embroidery of worldwide culture, as nearby customs find new crowds and appreciation around the world.

Additionally, sashets as specialty content makers and autonomous craftsmen have upset customary media outlets. Web-based features and computerized stages have made it more straightforward for these makers to contact worldwide crowds, testing the strength of Hollywood and other conventional social centers.

Difficulties and Concerns

While sashetization offers numerous potential open doors and advantages, it likewise raises a few difficulties and worries with regards to globalization.

Power Irregularity: The dispersion of force achieved by sashetization can make precariousness and vulnerability in global relations. As customary power structures are tested, there is a gamble of contentions and fights for control turning out to be more flighty and unstable.

Guideline and Administration: The quick ascent of sashets in different areas frequently dominates administrative systems and administration structures. State run administrations and global associations battle to adjust to the evolving scene, prompting issues, for example, information security concerns, administrative holes, and the potential for maltreatments of force.

Monetary Disparity: While sashetization can prompt financial development and advancement, it can likewise worsen monetary imbalance. More modest substances might not have the assets to follow guidelines or contend on a level battleground, prompting worries about restraining infrastructures and out of line rivalry.

Social Homogenization: The worldwide reach of sashets, especially in the computerized domain, can likewise prompt social homogenization. As specific thoughts, patterns, and social items gain worldwide unmistakable quality, there is a gamble of dissolving neighborhood societies and customs.

5.1 Consumer Behavior and Preferences

Customer conduct and inclinations are at the center of present day showcasing and business systems. Understanding what drives customers to pursue specific decisions and creating items and administrations that line up with their inclinations is essential for outcome in the present cutthroat commercial center. This article dives into the mind boggling domain of buyer conduct, revealing insight into the different elements that impact choices and the manners by which organizations can adjust to meet purchaser inclinations.

The Purchaser Dynamic Cycle

Buyer conduct can be seen as a cycle that includes a few phases, each impacted by a large number of elements. While this cycle can change from one individual to another and item to item, it by and large incorporates the accompanying stages:

Issue Acknowledgment: The cycle starts when a customer perceives a need or issue. This acknowledgment can be set off by inner elements (e.g., craving) or outer variables (e.g., promoting).

Data Search: When a need is perceived, purchasers frequently look for data to assist them with pursuing a choice. They might assemble data from different sources, including companions, family, online audits, and promoting.

Assessment of Choices: Subsequent to social occasion data, buyers assess various choices or brands. This assessment might include looking at costs, quality, highlights, and different properties.

Buy Choice: In view of their assessment, customers settle on a buy choice. Notwithstanding, this choice might be affected by factors like accessibility, value limits, or suggestions from companions.

Post-Buy Conduct: After the buy, purchasers survey their fulfillment with the item or administration. Their degree of fulfillment can impact future purchasing choices and verbal exchange suggestions.

Factors Affecting Purchaser Conduct

Social Variables: Culture, subculture, and social class fundamentally influence shopper conduct. Various societies have particular qualities, convictions, and customs that influence inclinations. Subcultures, like strict or ethnic gatherings, can likewise impact decisions, as can social class, which frequently directs utilization designs.

Social Variables: Social elements incorporate reference gatherings, family, and social jobs. Buyers might be affected by the feelings and ways of behaving of their reference gatherings, and relational peculiarities can shape buying choices. Moreover, a singular's social jobs (e.g., parent, understudy, proficient) can influence what they purchase.

Individual Elements: Individual variables envelop age, life cycle stage, occupation, and financial circumstance. These factors influence an individual's requirements and purchasing limit. For example, a youthful grown-up may focus on innovation devices, while a retired person could zero in on movement and relaxation.

Mental Elements: Mental variables envelop inspiration, discernment, learning, convictions, and perspectives. Inspiration drives shoppers to satisfy explicit necessities, while insight decides how they decipher data. Learning shapes customer information, and convictions and perspectives impact inclinations. For instance, a wellbeing cognizant individual might have an inspirational perspective toward natural food varieties.

Situational Variables: Situational factors connect with the particular conditions where a buy is made. These incorporate the actual climate (store design, lighting, music), social climate (presence of others), and fleeting variables (season of day, earnestness). A very much planned store design, for example, can impact purchasing choices.

Advertising Blend: The showcasing blend involves the four Ps: Item, Value, Spot, and Advancement. Organizations can shape purchaser inclinations through item configuration, valuing methodologies, dissemination channels, and promoting efforts. Powerful advancement, specifically, can make mindfulness and impact purchaser insights.

On the web and Computerized Impacts: In the advanced age, online stages and virtual entertainment assume a huge part in forming purchaser conduct. Shoppers depend on web-based audits, proposals, and forces to be reckoned with to settle on buying choices. Organizations should lay out areas of strength for a presence and deal with their standing on computerized stages.

Feelings and Motivation: Feelings frequently assume a critical part in buyer conduct. Motivation buys, driven by profound reactions, can be impacted by factors like feel, item bundling, or the shopping experience. A very much planned, outwardly engaging item can set off certain feelings and lead to indiscreet purchasing choices.

Purchaser Inclinations: The Quest for Personalization

Purchaser inclinations are the particular decisions and tastes that people have while choosing items or administrations. Inclinations can differ broadly from one individual to another, making it trying for organizations to take care of assorted client needs. In any case, there is a developing pattern towards personalization in showcasing and item improvement.

Customization: Numerous shoppers esteem items and administrations that can be redone to their particular inclinations. This could include customized item proposals in view of past way of behaving (e.g., Amazon's item ideas) or permitting clients to tailor specific item includes (e.g., modifying the shade of a cell phone case).

Designated Showcasing: Advances in information examination and computerized promoting have empowered organizations to target customers with profoundly customized publicizing. By dissecting shopper conduct and segment information, organizations can convey advertisements that are bound to resound with individual inclinations.

Item Assortment: Offering an extensive variety of item choices can take special care of different purchaser inclinations. This procedure is obvious in ventures like design, where retailers give numerous styles, sizes, and varieties to suit different preferences.

Client Created Content: Empowering clients to produce content, like surveys and tributes, can assist with building trust and impact the inclinations of expected purchasers. Positive client created content can make a good impression of an item or administration.

Criticism and Reviews: Get-together input straightforwardly from shoppers through studies and input structures can give important experiences into their inclinations. This information can direct item improvement and promoting methodologies.

Moral and Supportable Decisions: A rising number of purchasers are settling on decisions in light of moral and manageability contemplations. Brands that line up with buyers' qualities and give eco-accommodating or morally obtained items can acquire an upper hand.

Challenges in Getting it and Adjusting to Inclinations

Information Security Concerns: Gathering and involving shopper information for personalization can raise protection concerns. Organizations should explore severe guidelines and acquire customers' trust by straightforwardly dealing with their information.

Adjusting Assortment and Intricacy: Offering such a large number of choices can overpower buyers, prompting choice weariness. Finding some kind of harmony among assortment and straightforwardness is fundamental.

Evolving Inclinations: Customer inclinations can be liquid and dependent on future developments, making it trying for organizations to stay aware of advancing preferences and patterns.

Market Immersion: In profoundly aggressive business sectors, it tends to be hard for organizations to separate their contributions in light of purchaser inclinations alone.

5.2 Market Expansion Strategies

Market extension systems are fundamental for organizations hoping to develop and expand their piece of the pie. Whether an organization is trying to enter new geological business sectors, target different client portions, or enhance its item contributions, having a thoroughly examined market development system is vital. In this article, we will investigate different market extension procedures, their advantages, and contemplations for effective execution.

1. Geographic Extension

Venturing into new topographical business sectors is one of the most widely recognized methodologies for development. It includes entering districts, nations, or urban communities where an organization's items or administrations are not right now accessible. This technique can take a few structures:

Worldwide Extension: Going past homegrown boundaries to arrive at global business sectors. Organizations like Coca-Cola and McDonald's have effectively executed worldwide extension techniques.

Local Extension: Zeroing in on unambiguous districts or adjoining nations prior to handling a more extensive global market. For example, a dress retailer could venture into adjoining nations prior to focusing on far off business sectors.

Advantages of Geographic Extension:

Expansion: Entering new business sectors can assist with spreading risk. Financial variances or political precariousness in one district might not have as serious an effect on the off chance that the business works in different business sectors.

Expanded Income: Getting to new client bases can prompt higher deals and income development.

Economies of Scale: Extending can prompt expense efficiencies, especially assuming creation volumes increment and dispersion networks become more effective.

Contemplations for Geographic Development:

Statistical surveying: Completely research target markets to grasp buyer inclinations, nearby rivalry, and administrative necessities.

Planned operations and Inventory network: Guarantee that the store network can uphold extension. Defers underway or appropriation can hurt the organization's standing.

Social Variation: Be ready to adjust to nearby societies and purchaser ways of behaving. This might include tweaking items or advertising techniques.

2. **Market Division**

Market division includes focusing on unambiguous client fragments with items or administrations custom-made to their requirements and inclinations. Rather than attempting to speak to a wide crowd, an organization distinguishes particular gatherings of clients and makes contributions that reverberate with each section.

Advantages of Market Division:

Further developed Client Commitment: Fitting items and advertising to explicit client portions can prompt higher commitment and transformation rates.

Expanded Unwaveringness: Meeting the special necessities of various client gatherings can encourage brand dependability and client maintenance.

Higher Overall revenues: Clients might pay a premium for items or administrations that definitely match their prerequisites.

Contemplations for Market Division:

Portion Recognizable proof: Cautiously distinguish and characterize client fragments in view of variables like socioeconomics, conduct, and inclinations.

Item Customization: Foster items or administrations that line up with each fragment's requirements. This might include varieties in elements, estimating, or promoting informing.

Asset Allotment: Apportion assets actually to reach and serve each portion. Various sections might require different showcasing efforts or circulation channels.

3. **Item Enhancement**

Flat Expansion: Adding items or administrations that are connected with the current contributions. For instance, a wellness hardware producer could begin creating wellness clothing.

Vertical Enhancement: Venturing into various phases of the inventory network. An eatery network could begin its own food creation or conveyance.

Related Expansion: Venturing into items or administrations that are connected with the center business yet not straight-forwardly tied. A hardware retailer could begin offering home robotization administrations.

Inconsequential Broadening: Venturing into altogether new and irrelevant businesses. A combination could claim organizations in areas as different as energy, media, and retail.

Advantages of Item Expansion:

Diminished Hazard: An assorted item portfolio can assist with moderating gamble by spreading it across various product offerings or ventures.

Income Development: New items can take advantage of existing client bases or set out open doors to draw in new clients.

Upper hand: Enhancing items can give a strategic advantage by offering a more extensive scope of arrangements than contenders.

Contemplations for Item Expansion:

Statistical surveying: Completely research the market for the new item or administration to guarantee there is request and to figure out the cutthroat scene.

Asset Designation: Consider the assets expected for improvement, creation, advertising, and appropriation of the new contribution.

Brand Consistency: Guarantee that the new items line up with the organization's image and fundamental beliefs.

4. **Consolidations and Acquisitions (M&A)**

Consolidations and acquisitions include one organization purchasing or converging with one more organization to grow its market presence, get new capacities, or enter new business sectors. M&A procedures can be ordered into the accompanying kinds:

Even Mix: Obtaining or converging with an immediate rival in a similar industry to grow piece of the pie and decrease contest.

Vertical Mix: Extending command over the inventory network by obtaining providers or merchants.

Aggregate Enhancement: Securing organizations in irrelevant ventures to differentiate the business portfolio.

Advantages of M&A:

Quick Development: M&A can prompt quick development by gaining laid out client bases and income streams.

Admittance to Assets: Obtaining organizations can give admittance to new advances, ability, or dissemination channels.

Market Passage: M&A can be an effective method for entering new business sectors without beginning without any preparation.

Contemplations for M&A:

A reasonable level of effort: Completely survey the monetary wellbeing, tasks, and social attack of the objective organization.

Coordination Difficulties: Effectively incorporating the procured organization's activities, frameworks, and work force can be intricate and requires cautious preparation.

Administrative and Legitimate Contemplations: Know about administrative prerequisites and lawful ramifications related with M&A exchanges.

5. **Diversifying and Permitting**

Diversifying and permitting are techniques that permit a business to extend without critical capital venture. These methodologies include conceding outsiders (franchisees or licensees) the option to utilize the organization's image, items, or administrations in return for charges or sovereignties.

Diversifying: Franchisees work their own organizations utilizing the franchisor's image, plan of action, and emotionally supportive networks. Models incorporate inexpensive food chains like McDonald's and retail outlets like The UPS Store.

Permitting: Permitting permits outsiders to utilize an organization's protected innovation, like brand names or licenses, to create and sell items or administrations. For instance, a dress brand might permit its logo to be utilized on different product.

Advantages of Diversifying and Permitting:

Quick Extension: Diversifying and authorizing can prompt fast market infiltration, as franchisees and licensees contribute their cash-flow to lay out and work areas.

Decreased Hazard: Franchisees and licensees bear a large part of the monetary gamble, permitting the parent organization to extend without huge capital venture.

Brand Expansion: Permitting can broaden a brand's venture into new item classifications or businesses.

Contemplations for Diversifying and Permitting:

Brand Control: Keep up with command over the brand to guarantee consistency and safeguard its standing.

Backing and Preparing: Give satisfactory preparation and backing to franchisees and licensees to guarantee they stick to mark principles.

Legitimate Arrangements: Lay out clear lawful arrangements that frame the freedoms as well as expectations of the two players.

6. **Advanced Development**

Internet business: Growing deals through web-based commercial centers, sites, and versatile applications. Organizations like Amazon and Alibaba have effectively utilized internet business systems.

Computerized Stages: Utilizing advanced stages to associate with clients and proposition administrations. Models incorporate web-based features like Netflix and ride-sharing stages like Uber.

SaaS (Programming as a Help): Offering programming applications and administrations through the cloud. Organizations like Microsoft and Salesforce have utilized SaaS to grow their client base.

Advantages of Advanced Development:

Worldwide Reach: Computerized extension can immediately interface organizations with a worldwide crowd, eliminating geological restrictions.

Cost Proficiency: Working carefully frequently requires lower above costs than conventional physical activities.

Versatility: Computerized stages can scale rapidly to oblige developing client bases.

Contemplations for Computerized Extension:

Computerized Advertising: Powerful advanced showcasing is fundamental to draw in and hold advanced clients. Put resources into techniques like website streamlining (Web optimization), online entertainment promoting, and pay-per-click publicizing.

Client Experience: Give a phenomenal client experience across computerized channels, as this can fundamentally affect consumer loyalty and maintenance.

Information Security: Execute hearty information safety efforts to safeguard client information and keep up with trust.

5.3 Innovation and Entrepreneurship

Development and business venture are two strong drivers of monetary development, cultural advancement, and the change of enterprises. They are firmly interlaced and significantly affect the worldwide economy. In this article, we will investigate the ideas of advancement and business, their significance, their relationship, and their job in molding what's in store.

Characterizing Advancement and Business venture

Development alludes to the most common way of making and executing groundbreaking thoughts, strategies, items, or administrations that outcome in a huge improvement or progression. It can take different structures, including mechanical leap forwards, process enhancements, plan of action developments, and effective fixes to existing issues. Advancement can happen in any area, from medical care and innovation to assembling and money.

Business venture, then again, is the demonstration of distinguishing open doors and stepping up and make and grow another undertaking or put up advancement for sale to the public. Business people are people who will proceed with reasonable courses of action, prepare assets, and seek after their vision to lay out and deal with a business. Business isn't restricted to new companies; it can likewise include rejuvenating existing organizations or driving change inside laid out associations.

The Exchange Among Development and Business venture

Advancement and business are profoundly interlaced and commonly building up. Business visionaries frequently act as the impetuses for advancement by recognizing market holes, neglected requirements, or failures. They then, at that point, step up and foster inventive arrangements and offer them for sale to the public.

On the other hand, development gives business people the instruments and chances to separate themselves from contenders, make novel offers, and upset laid out enterprises. Fruitful business people are in many cases the individuals who can use development really to acquire an upper hand.

Significance of Development and Business

Financial Development: Advancement and business are key drivers of monetary development. They make new businesses, create work open doors, and add to expanded efficiency and Gross domestic product development.

Work Creation: Business prompts the production of new organizations, which, thusly, creates business open doors. New companies and private ventures are in many cases critical causes of occupation creation in economies all over the planet.

Seriousness: Developments in items, administrations, and plans of action improve a country's intensity on the worldwide stage. Countries that energize advancement and business will quite often have strong economies and flourishing ventures.

Cultural Advancement: Developments in regions like medical care, schooling, and sustainable power can possibly address a portion of society's most squeezing difficulties, working on the personal satisfaction for a great many individuals.

Mechanical Progression: Innovative endeavors frequently drive mechanical headways. Organizations like Apple, Tesla, and Amazon have altered their particular businesses through creative items and administrations.

Difficulties and Boundaries

Monetary Assets: Admittance to financing is a typical hindrance, particularly for new companies. Business visionaries frequently battle to tie down cash-flow to transform their thoughts into the real world.

Administrative Obstacles: Complex guidelines and regulatory cycles can impede business and development, especially in profoundly managed enterprises like medical services and money.

Market Contest: Soaked markets and extraordinary rivalry can make it trying for new business people to acquire a traction and accomplish market separation.

Hazard avoidance: Numerous people and associations are risk-loath and reluctant to embrace novel thoughts or put resources into dubious endeavors.

Licensed innovation: Safeguarding protected innovation privileges can be intricate and exorbitant, making it hard for trailblazers to defend their manifestations.

Development Models

Open Development: Begat by Henry Chesbrough, the open advancement model underscores joint effort with outer accomplices, including clients, providers, and different associations, to create and execute novel thoughts. It perceives that significant thoughts can emerge out of sources past an organization's interior Research and development endeavors.

Troublesome Advancement: Created by Clayton Christensen, the hypothesis of problematic development sets that laid out organizations can be disturbed by inventive newbies who target underserved markets with easier, more reasonable arrangements. Problematic developments frequently start as specialty contributions yet in the end gain standard acknowledgment.

Steady Advancement: This approach centers around making continuous enhancements to existing items, administrations, or cycles. It is safer than extremist development and is frequently used to keep an organization's serious situation on the lookout.

Configuration Thinking: Plan thinking puts areas of strength for an on understanding end-clients' necessities and encounters. It includes a human-focused way to deal with critical thinking, with iterative ideation and prototyping.

Lean Startup: The lean startup approach, promoted by Eric Ries, advocates for building least practical items (MVPs) to test speculations and accumulate criticism from clients prior to putting vigorously in item advancement.

Advancement Environments

Advancement doesn't occur in seclusion; it flourishes inside biological systems that encourage imagination, joint effort, and the trading of thoughts. Development biological systems regularly incorporate a mix of the accompanying parts:

Pioneering Society: A culture that supports risk-taking, trial and error, and gaining from disappointment is fundamental for encouraging development and business.

Training and Exploration Foundations: Colleges and examination focuses assume a significant part in producing new information and innovations that can be popularized.

Startup Environment: Lively startup networks, with admittance to hatcheries, gas pedals, and funding, can offer the fundamental help for business people.

Government Arrangements: Government strategies and motivators, for example, tax cuts and awards, can empower development and business venture.

Admittance to Subsidizing: Admittance to different wellsprings of financing, including private supporters, investors, and government awards, is imperative for new businesses and inventive undertakings.

Coordinated effort Organizations: Cooperation between industry players, research establishments, and new companies can work with the exchange of information and innovation.

Development and Business venture Practically speaking

Tesla, Inc.: Tesla, drove by Elon Musk, has upset the car business through electric vehicles and environmentally friendly power arrangements. The organization's inventive way to deal with battery innovation, independent driving, and energy stockpiling has disturbed the customary car area.

Macintosh Inc.: Mac is known for its determined obligation to advancement, creating famous items like the iPhone, iPad, and MacBook. Its environment of equipment, programming, and administrations has re-imagined buyer innovation.

Biotechnology New companies: New businesses in the biotechnology area are driving noteworthy developments in medical services, including quality treatment, customized medication, and CRISPR quality altering.

Fintech Disruptors: Fintech new companies like Square, Stripe, and Robinhood have changed the monetary administrations industry, offering computerized installment arrangements, internet contributing stages, and elective financial administrations.

Environmentally friendly power: Advancements in environmentally friendly power innovations, like sunlight based chargers and wind turbines, are driving the change to cleaner and more economical energy sources.

5.4 Cultural Exchange and Adaptation

Social trade and transformation are two powerful cycles that assume an essential part in our interconnected world. They include the sharing of social components, like traditions, customs, dialects, and values, among various gatherings and people. These cycles span social partitions as well as add to the improvement and advancement of social orders. In this article, we will investigate the meaning of social trade and variation, their effect on people and social orders, and the difficulties and advantages they bring.

Social Trade: An Entryway to Understanding

Travel and The travel industry: Voyagers frequently drench themselves in the way of life of the objections they visit, encountering nearby practices, cooking, and customs.

Language Getting the hang of: Learning another dialect is a significant type of social trade, as it permits people to speak with individuals from various phonetic foundations.

Worldwide Training: Concentrating abroad or facilitating global understudies encourages culturally diverse comprehension and opens people to various schooling systems and viewpoints.

Social Celebrations and Occasions: Occasions that exhibit music, dance, workmanship, and cooking from different societies give chances to individuals to appreciate and find out about various customs.

Business and Exchange: Globalization has prompted expanded social trade in the business world, as organizations work in different business sectors and team up with global accomplices.

Meaning of Social Trade:

Advancing Comprehension: Social trade encourages sympathy, resistance, and a more profound comprehension of various societies. It separates generalizations and biases by permitting individuals to see the world according to numerous points of view.

Upgrading Social Mindfulness: Openness to various traditions and customs advances people's social mindfulness and expands their perspectives. It empowers appreciation for the variety of human encounters.

Building Associations: Social trade fabricates relational associations and global connections. Kinships framed through social trades can prompt coordinated efforts and associations that rise above borders.

Self-improvement: Social trade provokes people to get out of their usual ranges of familiarity, adjust to new conditions, and foster critical thinking abilities. It frequently prompts self-awareness and expanded fearlessness.

Social Variation: Exploring the Multicultural World

Absorption: In this procedure, people embrace the social standards and practices of the prevailing society, frequently to the degree that they lose their unique social character.

Combination: Joining includes keeping up with one's unique culture while additionally embracing parts of the new culture. It accentuates the concurrence of various social characters.

Partition: Detachment happens when people oppose taking on the new culture and on second thought disconnect themselves inside their own social local area.

Minimization: Underestimation includes people feeling distanced from both their unique culture and the new culture. It is frequently connected with sensations of rejection.

Effect of Social Variation:

Character Development: Social variation assumes a critical part in forming people's personalities. They might explore a complicated mix of social components, prompting a complex personality that reflects both their legacy and their took on culture.

Social Amalgamation: Social transformation can bring about the union of social components, making new types of social articulation and advancement. For instance, combination food consolidates fixings and cooking strategies from various culinary customs.

Social Clash: Social variation can some of the time lead to clashes as people or gatherings wrestle with contrasts in values, standards, and assumptions. These contentions can appear in different ways, from generational conflicts to personality emergencies.

Cultural Variety: In multicultural social orders, social transformation adds to the variety and wealth of networks. It unites individuals from different foundations, advancing the structure holding the system together.

Difficulties and Advantages of Social Trade and Transformation

Challenges:

Social Shock: People encountering another culture may at first face culture shock, described by sensations of confusion, tension, and disappointment as they conform to new traditions and standards.

Language Hindrances: Language contrasts can be a critical obstacle to powerful social trade and transformation. Language capability is much of the time fundamental for significant correspondence and mix.

Character Battles: People exploring numerous social personalities might wrestle with inquiries of having a place and credibility. They might encounter a feeling of social vagueness or struggle.

Generalizing and Bias: Social trade can once in a while support generalizations or lead to biased mentalities on the off chance that not drew nearer with a receptive outlook and a readiness to learn.

Benefits:

Social Advancement: Social trade and variation enhance people's lives by presenting them to new encounters, information, and viewpoints. This social advancement prompts self-awareness and more noteworthy social mindfulness.

Worldwide Citizenship: Social trade cultivates a feeling of worldwide citizenship, underlining our interconnectedness and shared liability regarding tending to worldwide difficulties.

Financial Open doors: Social trade can animate monetary open doors through the travel industry, exchange, and worldwide coordinated efforts, helping the two people and networks.

Harmony and Tact: Social trade can be an amazing asset for discretion and compromise, advancing comprehension and participation between countries.

True Models

Jazz Music: Jazz is a classification that arose in the US yet has gone through broad social transformation and trade. It has been embraced and adjusted in assorted societies around the world, bringing about exceptional varieties of jazz music in places like New Orleans, Paris, and Havana.

Food Culture: The combination of culinary customs is obvious in dishes like sushi burritos (a combination of Japanese and Mexican cooking styles), showing the way that social variation can prompt imaginative and scrumptious results.

Language and Writing: Abstract works like "100 Years of Isolation" by Gabriel García Márquez, initially written in Spanish, have been converted into various dialects, permitting perusers from various social foundations to get to and see the value in the writer's work.

Global Schooling: Concentrate abroad projects furnish understudies with the chance to take part in social trade and transformation. These encounters frequently lead to self-awareness, extended perspectives, and deep rooted associations.

6

Chapter6

Case Studies

Contextual analyses are a generally used research technique across different disciplines, filling in as an important device for examining complex peculiarities, all things considered, settings. Whether in business, brain science, medication, or sociologies, contextual analyses offer scientists a chance to dive profound into explicit circumstances, investigate the complexities of human way of behaving, and make significant determinations. In this extensive examination, we will dive into the universe of contextual analyses, looking at their motivation, types, strategy, benefits, and limits from the perspective of functional models.

1. Understanding Contextual analyses

1.1 Definition and Reason

A contextual investigation can be characterized as a top to bottom assessment of a specific subject, frequently inside its genuine setting, meaning to comprehend and decipher its intricacies. The main role of a contextual investigation is to acquire bits of knowledge, create speculations, or give answers for issues, all while protecting the all encompassing nature of the subject being scrutinized.

1.2 Sorts of Contextual investigations

1. **Unmistakable Contextual investigations:** These try to give a nitty gritty record of a specific peculiarity or subject, permitting perusers to acquire a complete comprehension of the case.
2. **Exploratory Contextual investigations:** These intend to investigate new regions, create theories, and accumulate primer information that can illuminate future examination.
3. **Illustrative Contextual analyses:** These are led to make sense of causal connections between factors or occasions, frequently involving existing speculations or systems as a premise.
4. **Instrumental Contextual analyses:** In instrumental contextual analyses, the actual case isn't the essential concentration; rather, it fills in as a way to explore a more extensive peculiarity.
5. **Natural Contextual investigations:** Here, the case is innately intriguing or novel, and scientists concentrate on it for the well-being of its own.

II. Procedure of Contextual analyses
2.1 Information Assortment

1. **Meetings:** Directing organized or semi-organized interviews with key people engaged with the case.
2. **Perceptions:** Deliberate and member perceptions to accumulate direct data.
3. **Report Examination:** Investigating records, records, and documented materials connected with the case.
4. **Overviews:** Controlling reviews to accumulate quantitative information, when fundamental.

2.2 Information Investigation

Whenever information is gathered, it goes through thorough investigation, frequently utilizing procedures like topical coding, content examination, or example acknowledgment. Scientists endeavor to distinguish key subjects, examples, and connections inside the information, helping with the improvement of a complete comprehension of the case.

III. Benefits of Contextual investigations

3.1 Profundity and Wealth

One of the essential benefits of contextual analyses is their capacity to give top to bottom experiences into complex peculiarities. Specialists can investigate the complexities of a specific subject, taking into account numerous factors and context oriented factors.

3.2 Genuine Setting

Contextual analyses are directed, in actuality, settings, making them environmentally legitimate. This context oriented extravagance permits specialists to all the more likely comprehend how a subject works inside its regular habitat.

3.3 Speculation Age

Contextual analyses frequently act as an establishment for producing speculations or hypotheses that can be tried in more extensive examination attempts. They offer a beginning stage for additional examination.

3.4 Adaptability

Contextual investigations are adaptable and versatile to different exploration questions and trains. Scientists can fit their way to deal with suit the particular necessities of their review.

IV. Contextual analyses in Different Disciplines

4.1 Business and The board

Contextual analyses are broadly utilized in the business and the board fields to examine organizations, dynamic cycles, and key preparation. The Harvard Business college case strategy is a renowned model, zeroing in on true business situations.

4.2 Brain research

In brain research, contextual analyses are instrumental in figuring out human way of behaving and mental cycles. Sigmund Freud's psychoanalytic contextual investigations, like the examination of Little Hans, stay persuasive.

4.3 Medication

Clinical contextual analyses are critical for archiving interesting ailments, treatment results, and patient accounts. They add to clinical information, analysis, and treatment procedures.

4.4 Training

In training, contextual analyses are utilized to analyze showing strategies, understudy execution, and instructive approaches. They offer important experiences for working on instructive practices.

V. Impediments of Contextual analyses

5.1 Absence of Generalizability

One of the essential impediments of contextual analyses is their restricted generalizability. Since they center around unambiguous cases, applying their discoveries to more extensive populaces or situations can challenge.

5.2 Subjectivity

The understanding of contextual investigation information can be emotional, affected by the specialist's predispositions and points of view. This subjectivity might prompt possible mistakes.

5.3 Time and Asset Serious

Contextual investigations can be tedious and asset serious, requiring broad information assortment and examination endeavors.

5.4 Moral Worries

Moral difficulties might emerge in the event that reviews, particularly while managing delicate subjects or circumstances. Scientists should explore these issues cautiously.

VI. Conspicuous Contextual analyses

6.1 The Stanford Jail Trial

Led by Philip Zimbardo in 1971, this scandalous brain science concentrate on researched the impacts of seen power in a reproduced jail climate. It uncovered the significant effect of situational factors on human way of behaving.

6.2 The Challenger Fiasco

The Space Transport Challenger fiasco in 1986 fills in as an exemplary contextual investigation in designing and morals. It analyzed the imperfect dynamic interaction that prompted the disastrous blast.

6.3 The Enron Embarrassment

The Enron embarrassment in the mid 2000s is a notable contextual investigation in corporate misrepresentation and morals. It shed light on the unscrupulous monetary acts of the Enron Enterprise and their broad outcomes.

6.4 The Rock Water Emergency

The Rock water emergency, which started in 2014, is a contextual investigation in general wellbeing and government disappointment. It featured the risks of lead-tainted water and the effect of insufficient government reaction.

6.1 Sashetization in Emerging Economies

Sashetization is a term that has acquired noticeable quality in conversations about the financial scene of arising economies. It alludes to the developing pattern of a rising working class, described by expanded extra cash, urbanization, and changing shopper inclinations. This peculiarity is reshaping the monetary and social texture of many emerging countries, with broad ramifications for organizations, legislatures, and society all in all. In this paper, we will investigate the idea of sashetization in arising economies, its causes, results, and the difficulties it presents.

1. Figuring out Sashetization

1.1 Definition

Sashetization is gotten from the Hindi word "sashet," and that signifies "favored" or "well-off." It depicts the course of a huge part of a populace progressing from lower-pay status to a higher financial class. This change is described by expanded pay levels, worked on expectations for everyday comforts, and a shift from provincial to metropolitan regions.

1.2 Reasons for Sashetization

1. **Monetary Development:** Hearty financial development and industrialization are key drivers of sashetization. These cycles set out work open doors, support pay levels, and work with the development of a working class.
2. **Urbanization:** Fast urbanization is a typical component of sashetization. As individuals move from rustic to metropolitan regions looking for better open doors, they frequently experience an expansion in pay and admittance to conveniences.
3. **Schooling:** Further developed admittance to training is instrumental in sashetization. An informed labor force will in general acquire higher salaries and is better prepared to partake in the cutting edge economy.
4. **Globalization:** The incorporation of arising economies into the worldwide market has extended open doors for exchange, speculation, and occupation creation, adding to sashetization.

II. Outcomes of Sashetization

2.1 Financial Development

Sashetization can animate financial development in arising economies. As the working class grows, there is an ascent in purchaser spending, expanded interest for labor and products, and a lift to nearby businesses.

2.2 Decrease of Pay Imbalance

At times, sashetization might prompt a decrease in pay imbalance, as a bigger working class arises. Notwithstanding, this impact can fluctuate contingent upon government strategies and the dispersion of riches.

2.3 Changing Utilization Examples

Sashetization frequently brings about changing customer inclinations. Individuals with higher livelihoods will quite often look for better quality items, administrations, and encounters, prompting shifts on the lookout.

2.4 Framework Advancement

Quick urbanization driven by sashetization might provoke state run administrations to put resources into foundation improvement, like transportation, lodging, and sterilization, to oblige the developing metropolitan populace.

2.5 Political Ramifications

The rise of a sizable working class can have political outcomes, as this gathering might request more prominent political portrayal, responsibility, and social administrations.

III. Difficulties of Sashetization

3.1 Pay Inconsistencies

While sashetization can lessen pay imbalance at times, it can likewise fuel incongruities in the event that not oversaw really. A few people might help more from monetary development, prompting a developing pay hole.

3.2 Natural Worries

The expanded utilization related with sashetization can come down on the climate. More prominent interest for assets, energy, and transportation can prompt natural corruption on the off chance that not joined by manageable practices.

3.3 Foundation Strain

Quick urbanization coming about because of sashetization can strain existing foundation. States might battle to give sufficient lodging, transportation, and sterilization administrations for the developing metropolitan populace.

3.4 Social Separation

The movement from country to metropolitan regions can bring about friendly disengagement, as people abandon customary networks and face difficulties adjusting to metropolitan life.

3.5 Political Unsteadiness

The requests of a thriving working class for political portrayal and responsibility can prompt political unsteadiness in the event that legislatures neglect to answer satisfactorily to these requests.

IV. Contextual analyses

4.1 India

India is much of the time refered to as an unmistakable illustration of sashetization. The nation has seen huge monetary development, urbanization, and the extension of its working class in late many years. This change has prompted expanded shopper spending, a thriving tech industry, and a developing administrations area. In any case, India additionally faces difficulties like pay imbalance, ecological debasement, and the requirement for broad framework advancement.

4.2 China

China's quick monetary development and urbanization have been joined by a gigantic sashetization process. The nation has encountered a momentous shift from an agrarian economy to a modern and innovative force to be reckoned with. This change has lifted millions out of destitution and made a prospering working class. China's administration has dealt with this cycle through essential preparation, yet it additionally faces difficulties like pay disparity and natural issues.

6.2Global Brands and Localization Efforts

In our undeniably interconnected world, worldwide brands have turned into an omnipresent piece of our day to day routines. From Coca-Cola to Apple, these brands are perceived and loved around the world. Be that as it may, making worldwide progress isn't just about extending come to; it's additionally about adjusting to neighborhood societies and inclinations. This exposition investigates the idea of worldwide brands and the basic job of restriction endeavors in their prosperity, diving into the difficulties and advantages of tracking down the sensitive harmony between worldwide consistency and nearby pertinence.

1. Figuring out Worldwide Brands

1.1 Definition

Worldwide brands are organizations or items that are perceived and regarded across borders, frequently inseparable from quality, dependability, and a steady brand picture. These brands rise above social, phonetic, and geographic limits, interesting to shoppers around the world.

1.2 Qualities

1. **Reliable Marking:** They keep a predictable brand personality, logo, and informing that resound generally.
2. **Extensive range:** Worldwide brands have a huge presence in numerous nations and locales.
3. **Multifaceted Allure:** They adjust to assorted societies while keeping up with their center image quintessence.
4. **Reliability:** Worldwide brands are seen as solid and top caliber, which cultivates purchaser trust.

II. Limitation Endeavors in Worldwide Brands

2.1 What is Confinement?

Restriction is the method involved with adjusting an item, administration, or showcasing effort to meet the social, phonetic, and administrative prerequisites of a particular market or district. It goes past interpretation and incorporates social subtleties, inclinations, and legitimate contemplations.

2.2 Why Restriction Matters

1. **Social Responsiveness:** It guarantees that items and informing line up with nearby traditions, values, and convictions, staying away from social slips up.
2. **Market Significance:** Confinement assists worldwide brands with staying applicable and interesting to neighborhood customers, expanding their odds of coming out on top.
3. **Administrative Consistence:** Various locales have shifting lawful prerequisites that worldwide brands should comply with.
4. **Upper hand:** Brands that successfully limit can outflank contenders by interfacing with purchasers on a more profound level.

III. Advantages of Restriction Endeavors

3.1 Upgraded Market Entrance

Confinement empowers worldwide brands to effectively infiltrate new business sectors. By adjusting to nearby preferences and inclinations, they can actually rival laid out neighborhood brands.

3.2 Better Client Commitment

Limited content and informing reverberate with shoppers on an individual level. This commitment cultivates steadfastness and support, as customers feel a real association with the brand.

3.3 Expanded Deals and Income

At the point when worldwide brands take care of neighborhood needs and inclinations, they can take advantage of a bigger client base, prompting expanded deals and income.

3.4 Brand Faithfulness

Viable restriction endeavors exhibit a brand's obligation to a locale, cultivating unwaveringness among customers who value the additional mile taken to address their issues.

IV. Difficulties of Confinement

4.1 Adjusting Worldwide Consistency and Neighborhood Significance

Quite possibly of the greatest test worldwide brands face is finding some kind of harmony between keeping a predictable worldwide picture and adjusting to neighborhood markets. Over-confinement can weaken the brand's character, while under-limitation can prompt social harshness.

4.2 Language and Social Subtleties

Dialects and societies are intricate, making precise restriction testing. Confounding social subtleties or mistranslations can prompt humiliating or hostile advertising botches.

4.3 Asset Force

Powerful restriction can be asset escalated, requiring interests in statistical surveying, interpretation administrations, and social specialists.

4.4 Overseeing Brand Value

Worldwide brands should cautiously deal with their image value while venturing into new business sectors. Bungles between brand values and neighborhood inclinations can harm the brand's standing.

V. Contextual analyses

5.1 McDonald's

McDonald's is an exemplary illustration of a worldwide brand that effectively executes restriction endeavors. While it keeps up with center menu things like the Huge Macintosh, it additionally offers district explicit things like the McSpicy Paneer in India and the Teriyaki Burger in Japan. Also, McDonald's adjusts its eatery stylistic layout and atmosphere to suit neighborhood inclinations.

5.2 Coca-Cola

Coca-Cola is another worldwide brand that succeeds at confinement. The organization fits its showcasing efforts to neighborhood societies and occasions while keeping the notable red name reliable. For instance, during Chinese New Year, Coca-Cola discharges exceptional version bottles with Chinese good tidings.

VI. Systems for Powerful Limitation

6.1 Far reaching Statistical surveying

Worldwide brands should put resources into exhaustive statistical surveying to grasp nearby purchaser ways of behaving, inclinations, and social subtleties.

6.2 Work together with Nearby Specialists

Joining forces with nearby specialists and social experts can give priceless bits of knowledge and assist with exploring complex social scenes.

6.3 Adaptability in Item Contributions

Keep a harmony between a worldwide menu and district explicit contributions to take special care of both neighborhood tastes and the brand's center character.

6.4 Reliable Brand Values

While adjusting to nearby societies, guarantee that the brand's guiding principle and mission stay predictable, supporting the brand's character.

6.3 Technology and Sashetization

Sashetization, the ascent of a prospering working class in arising economies, is generally entwined with innovation. The advanced upheaval, portrayed by the far reaching reception of cell phones, web availability, and computerized stages, has reshaped the financial scene of many agricultural countries. In this paper, we will investigate the significant effect of innovation on sashetization, looking at how computerized developments have sped up this groundbreaking system, and examining the open doors and difficulties that emerge thus.

1. ## The Advanced Transformation and Sashetization
   ### 1.1 The Computerized Separation

The computerized unrest plays had a critical impact in sashetization by connecting the computerized partition. In many arising economies, admittance to innovation was once restricted to a special minority, yet the far and wide accessibility of reasonable cell phones and web network has democratized admittance to data and potential open doors. This has empowered a critical piece of the populace to partake in the worldwide computerized economy.

1.2 Web based business and Market Access

One of the most recognizable effects of innovation on sashetization is the multiplication of web based business stages. Computerized commercial centers like Amazon, Alibaba, and Flipkart have opened up huge commercial centers, permitting purchasers in arising economies to get to a large number of items and administrations from around the world. This has extended shopper decisions as well as given open doors to nearby organizations to contact worldwide crowds.

1.3 Fintech and Monetary Incorporation

Monetary innovation, or fintech, has been instrumental in giving admittance to monetary administrations to beforehand unbanked or underbanked populaces. Portable banking, computerized wallets, and shared loaning stages have empowered people and private ventures in arising economies to deal with their funds all the more productively and access credit, adding to their monetary strengthening.

1.4 Internet based Schooling and Ability Improvement

The computerized insurgency has democratized instruction and expertise improvement. Web based learning stages, like Coursera, edX, and Khan Foundation, offer free or reasonable courses that permit people in arising economies to secure new abilities and information, improving their employability and pay procuring potential.

2. Open doors Emerging from Innovation Driven Sashetization

2.1 Monetary Development and Business

Sashetization energized by innovation has animated financial development in arising economies. The ascent of computerized business people and new companies has set out work open doors and supported advancement, adding to monetary turn of events.

2.2 Upgraded Market Access

Innovation has wiped out geological obstructions, empowering nearby organizations to get to worldwide business sectors. Little and medium-sized ventures (SMEs) in arising economies can now send out their items and administrations around the world, prompting expanded income and development.

2.3 Monetary Consideration

Fintech developments have made monetary administrations more open to a more extensive populace. This has prompted expanded reserve funds, venture, and generally monetary security among people and independent companies.

2.4 Ability Improvement and Employability

Online training and expertise advancement stages have engaged people to obtain new abilities and work on their employability. This, thusly, has prompted more lucrative open positions and professional success.

3. **Difficulties and Concerns**

3.1 Advanced Separation Inside Arising Economies

While innovation has spanned the computerized partition on a worldwide scale, differences actually exist inside arising economies. Country regions and underestimated networks frequently need admittance to solid web availability and computerized foundation, restricting their capacity to profit from sashetization.

3.2 Protection and Information Security

As innovation turns out to be more basic to day to day existence, worries about protection and information security have developed. Arising economies frequently need strong information insurance guidelines, leaving people powerless against information breaks and abuse.

3.3 Work Relocation

While innovation sets out work open doors, it can likewise prompt work relocation, especially in businesses that are vigorously dependent on difficult work. As robotization and computerized reasoning keep on progressing, dealing with the effect on the labor force turns into a huge test.

3.4 Network protection Dangers

The rising dependence on innovation uncovered people and organizations to network protection dangers, including cyberattacks and misrepresentation. Arising economies might miss the mark on assets and aptitude to battle these dangers actually.

4. **Contextual analyses**

4.1 China: Alibaba Gathering

Alibaba, established by Jack Mama, is a perfect representation of how innovation can drive sashetization. Alibaba's online business stages, for example, Taobao and Tmall, have changed the manner in which Chinese customers shop as well as given open doors to a large number of private ventures to flourish in the computerized commercial center. Moreover, Alibaba's monetary arm, Subterranean insect Gathering, offers advanced monetary administrations, adding to monetary consideration in China.

4.2 India: Advanced Installments

India has seen a huge ascent in computerized installments, because of drives like the Bound together Installments Connection point (UPI) and versatile wallet administrations like Paytm. These advancements have made it simpler for people to deal with their funds, execute carefully, and access credit, promoting sashetization in the country.

5. Strategy and Vital Contemplations

5.1 Crossing over the Advanced Gap

Legislatures and associations ought to focus on endeavors to connect the computerized partition inside their nations. Putting resources into computerized foundation, extending web network to underserved regions, and advancing advanced education are fundamental stages.

5.2 Information Security and Protection

Arising economies ought to establish strong information assurance regulations and guidelines to defend people's protection and information security. Building trust in the advanced biological system is urgent for economical sashetization.

5.3 Upskilling and Instruction

Advancing computerized proficiency and giving admittance to online training and expertise improvement assets can engage people to take part in the advanced economy completely.

5.4 Supporting Computerized Business

States can uphold computerized business by establishing a helpful administrative climate, offering motivators for new companies, and giving admittance to supporting and mentorship.

6.4 Cultural Preservation in the Age of Globalization

In the time of globalization, the world has become more inter-connected than any other time. The progression of thoughts, products, and data rises above borders, achieving phenomenal open doors and difficulties. In the midst of this quick change, one basic concern is the safeguarding of social legacy. Globalization, with its social homogeniza-tion propensities, represents an imposing test to the rich embroidery of customs, dialects, and customs that make up our different worldwide legacy. In this exposition, we will investigate the unpredictable connec-tion among globalization and social protection, looking at the powers at play, the techniques utilized to shield social

legacy, and the significance of finding some kind of harmony among custom and change.

1. **Globalization and Social Disintegration**
   ### 1.1 Social Homogenization
   Globalization has prompted the spread of predominant social stories, frequently determined by Western goals and values. This peculiarity, here and there alluded to as social colonialism, can minimize or eclipse nearby customs and practices.
   ### 1.2 Industrialism and Broad communications
   The worldwide reach of industrialism and broad communica-tions has made a "worldwide culture" described by normalized items, style, and media content. While this can cultivate a feeling of interconnectedness, it can likewise reduce the uniqueness of neighborhood societies.
   ### 1.3 Language Misfortune
   Globalization has been a main impetus behind the decay of nu-merous native dialects. As prevailing dialects, for example, English become more pervasive, the etymological variety of the world lessens, taking with it novel perspectives and social subtleties.
   ### 1.4 Urbanization
   The quick urbanization related with globalization frequently up-roots conventional networks and lifestyles. Conventional country

rehearses are progressively giving way to metropolitan ways of life, possibly disintegrating social legacy.

2. **Procedures for Social Protection**

2.1 Social Training

Social training assumes an essential part in saving legacy. Schools, exhibition halls, and social foundations can show the more youthful age their social roots, history, and customs, imparting a feeling of satisfaction and personality.

2.2 Social Documentation

Recording oral chronicles, reporting conventional practices, and filing relics are fundamental stages in saving social legacy. These endeavors guarantee that information is passed down to people in the future.

2.3 Language Rejuvenation

Endeavors to resuscitate and advance native dialects are critical for social conservation. Language is a critical transporter of social personality, and language renewal programs assist with keeping these customs alive.

2.4 Social Celebrations and Festivities

Social celebrations and festivities give a stage to networks to feature their customs, ceremonies, and expressions. These occasions can fortify social personality and empower the transmission of customs.

3. **The Significance of Social Conservation**

3.1 Social Variety

Social conservation is indispensable for keeping up with the world's rich social variety. Each culture contributes extraordinary points of view, information, and lifestyles to the worldwide embroidery.

3.2 Personality and Having a place

Saving social legacy builds up people's feeling of character and having a place. It gives a connection to their predecessors, roots, and a more profound comprehension of what their identity is.

3.3 Verifiable Inheritance

Social protection guarantees that the verifiable tradition of a local area or country isn't lost. It permits people in the future to gain from an earlier time and value the commitments of their progenitors.

3.4 Advancing Resilience and Understanding

An assorted social scene encourages resistance and understanding among various gatherings. Social protection can act as an extension for exchange and common regard.

4. Contextual investigations

4.1 Bhutan: Gross Public Bliss

Bhutan has sought after a one of a kind way to deal with social conservation through its idea of Gross Public Joy (GNH). The GNH system focuses on social safeguarding and natural maintainability as fundamental parts of the country's prosperity. Bhutan's emphasis on saving its particular social personality, remembering the utilization of the Bhutanese language for schools and media, has gathered worldwide consideration.

4.2 Japan: Theoretical Social Legacy

Japan's Theoretical Social Legacy framework perceives and protects conventional expressions, artworks, and ceremonies. Through this program, Japan has defended practices like Kabuki theater, conventional papermaking, and tea functions, guaranteeing that they keep on being gone down through ages.

5. Difficulties and Reactions

5.1 Social Assignment

Globalization has additionally prompted social apportionment, where components of one culture are acquired or imitated without legitimate comprehension or regard. This can prompt bending and commodification of social practices.

5.2 Monetary Tensions

Networks might confront monetary tensions to leave customary practices for additional beneficial, globalized other options. Thus, social conservation endeavors might require practical financial motivating forces.

5.3 Changing Qualities

As social orders develop, a few conventional practices might be considered obsolete or at this point not significant. Finding some kind of harmony between saving social legacy and embracing change can challenge.

6. Finding Some kind of harmony

6.1 Social Variation

Safeguarding social legacy doesn't mean opposing change out and out. Societies have consistently adjusted to new conditions, and this versatility is important for what makes them strong. The key is to adjust without losing the pith of one's social personality.

6.2 Intercultural Discourse

Advancing intercultural discourse cultivates understanding and appreciation between societies. Empowering discussions and trades between networks can assist with protecting customs while taking into consideration positive impacts from different societies.

6.3 Supportable Turn of events

Social protection endeavors ought to line up with manageable advancement objectives. Engaging people group monetarily and naturally can empower them to keep rehearsing their practices.

7 |

Chapter7

Challenges and Controversies

Difficulties and discussions are innate parts of human culture and progress. They shape our reality, brief conversations, and frequently lead to tremendous changes. In this complete investigation, we will dive into different difficulties and contentions traversing across various fields, like governmental issues, innovation, morals, and that's just the beginning. We will dissect the fundamental causes, suggestions, and likely answers for these intricate issues, offering a more profound comprehension of the complex idea of our contemporary world.

1. **Political Difficulties and Debates**
   1.1 Political Polarization
   Political polarization has become progressively articulated in numerous vote based systems, partitioning social orders along philosophical lines. This challenge blocks helpful discourse, smothers split the difference, and can subvert majority rule foundations.
   1.2 Populism
   The ascent of libertarian pioneers and developments all over the planet has started contention. Populism frequently takes advantage of famous discontent, representing a test to laid out political

standards and foundations.

1.3 Disinformation and Phony News

The spread of disinformation and phony news via online entertainment and different stages is a major problem. It subverts trust in organizations, contorts public discernment, and can impact political results.

1.4 Electing Uprightness

Guaranteeing the honesty of races stays a test in numerous nations. Debates connected with citizen concealment, manipulating, and unfamiliar obstruction can dissolve public confidence in the electing system.

2. Innovative Difficulties and Contentions

2.1 Security in the Computerized Age

The assortment and adaptation of individual information by tech monsters have raised critical security concerns. Adjusting the advantages of innovation with individual security privileges stays a mind boggling issue.

2.2 Computerized reasoning Morals

The fast headway of man-made reasoning (computer based intelligence) has prompted banters about its moral use, especially in regions like facial acknowledgment, independent weapons, and algorithmic predisposition.

2.3 Online protection Dangers

The rising recurrence and complexity of cyberattacks present critical difficulties. Safeguarding basic framework, individual information, and public safety from digital dangers is a continuous concern.

2.4 Tech Restraining infrastructures

Tech organizations with immense market power have confronted investigation for likely antitrust infringement. The debate encompassing their impact in different areas features the requirement for administrative activity.

3. Moral Difficulties and Debates

3.1 Environmental Change

Environmental change is a worldwide moral test that prompts banters about liability, value, and the critical requirement for natural activity. Discussions encompassing environment strategies and worldwide participation persevere.

3.2 Hereditary Designing

Progressions in hereditary designing raise moral difficulties, including worries about fashioner children, quality altering, and the potential for unseen side-effects.

3.3 Bioethics

Issues like killing, organ transplantation, and clinical trial and error keep on inciting moral contentions in the field of medical care and biotechnology.

3.4 Basic entitlements

Banters about basic entitlements and government assistance, including plant cultivating, creature testing, and the utilization of creatures in diversion, challenge society's moral qualities and practices.

4. Social Difficulties and Debates

4.1 Social Disparity

Augmenting pay and abundance imbalance present huge cultural difficulties. Discussions over tax collection, social wellbeing nets, and abundance rearrangement highlight the requirement for evenhanded strategies.

4.2 Movement

Movement is a petulant issue in numerous nations. Discusses focus on line security, outcast resettlement, and the monetary and social effect of migration.

4.3 Racial Shamefulness

The worldwide development against racial shamefulness, set off by occasions, for example, the People of color Matter fights, features the continuous battle against foundational prejudice and police savagery.

4.4 Orientation Uniformity

Orientation uniformity stays a test, with contentions encompassing issues like the orientation pay hole, working environment provocation, and admittance to conceptive privileges.

5. **Worldwide Difficulties and Discussions**

5.1 Worldwide Wellbeing Emergencies

The Coronavirus pandemic has uncovered shortcomings in worldwide wellbeing framework and raised contentions over antibody conveyance, travel limitations, and global participation.

5.2 Movement and Dislodging

Huge scope relocation and dislodging because of struggles, environmental change, and monetary shakiness are worldwide difficulties that brief discussions about compassionate reactions and migration approaches.

5.3 Atomic Expansion

The spread of atomic weapons stays a critical worldwide concern. Discussions over demobilization endeavors and peace treaties continue.

5.4 Worldwide Exchange and Monetary Reliance

Issues connected with exchange lopsided characteristics, protectionism, and financial reliance between countries keep on being a wellspring of strain and discussion in the worldwide field.

6. **Difficulties and Contentions in Science and Medication**

6.1 Immunization Aversion

Immunization reluctance has turned into a significant test in general wellbeing. Contentions encompassing immunization wellbeing, falsehood, and commands influence endeavors to accomplish group invulnerability.

6.2 Moral Issues in Medical services

Clinical morals issues, like finish of-life choices, asset assignment during emergencies, and the utilization of exploratory medicines, present complex difficulties for medical care experts and policymakers.

6.3 Logical Offense

Contentions connected with logical unfortunate behavior, including deceitful examination, copyright infringement, and irreconcilable circumstances, challenge the trustworthiness of logical information.

6.4 Arising Advancements

Arising advances, as CRISPR quality altering and human cloning, raise moral and moral difficulties that require cautious thought and guideline.

7. Contentions and Their Effect

7.1 Media and Public Insight

Media assumes a huge part in molding contentions and public discernment. How issues are outlined and detailed can impact popular assessment and strategy results.

7.2 Political Direction

Discussions frequently influence political navigation. Public tension, support, and preparation can prompt arrangement changes or official changes.

7.3 Social Developments

Numerous social developments, like social liberties, natural activism, and LGBTQ+ freedoms, have risen up out of contentions, driving social change and progress.

7.4 Global Relations

Contentions in worldwide relations, including disagreements about region, exchange, and common freedoms, can strain political relations and even lead to struggle.

8. Exploring Difficulties and Debates

8.1 Decisive Reasoning and Media Education

Advancing decisive reasoning and media proficiency is fundamental during a time of data over-burden. Outfitting people with the abilities to survey data's dependability and predisposition can assist with countering disinformation.

8.2 Discourse and Split the difference

In tending to political polarization and social division, open and helpful exchange is essential. Empowering split the difference and figuring out something worth agreeing on can connect philosophical partitions.

8.3 Moral Structures

Creating moral structures and rules for arising innovations, medical care, and different fields can give an establishment to tending to moral difficulties.

8.4 Worldwide Participation

Worldwide difficulties, for example, environmental change and pandemics, require global collaboration and multilateral methodologies. Strategy and worldwide administration are essential devices for resolving these issues.

7.1 Cultural Appropriation and Identity Loss

Social assignment is an idea that has acquired critical consideration and examination as of late. It alludes to the reception, frequently by predominant societies, of components from minimized or minority societies without legitimate grasping, regard, or affirmation. This peculiarity brings up significant issues about the conservation of social character and legacy. In this exposition, we will dig into the complex issues encompassing social apportionment, looking at its suggestions, causes, and the subsequent personality misfortune that minimized networks might insight.

1. Figuring out Social Appointment
1.1 Definition

Social allotment is the demonstration of taking or acquiring components from another culture, like dress, music, images, customs, or language, frequently without consent or understanding, and involving them for one's own motivations. It can appear in different structures, including style, craftsmanship, language, music, and, surprisingly, culinary practices.

1.2 Qualification from Social Trade

Social apportionment is particular from social trade, which includes a deferential and equal dividing of social components among various gatherings, frequently prompting common enhancement. Social allotment, then again, commonly happens inside a power irregularity, where the appropriating society holds more impact or honor.

2. Reasons for Social Allocation

2.1 Absence of Mindfulness

One of the essential drivers of social allocation is an absence of mindfulness or figuring out about the social importance and setting of the acquired components. Obliviousness or lack of concern can prompt the neglectful reception of social images.

2.2 Commercialization

The design and media outlets, specifically, have been censured for commercializing social components for benefit without recognizing their beginnings or regarding their social importance.

2.3 Power Elements

Social assignment frequently happens inside the setting of force lopsided characteristics. Prevailing societies might suitable from underestimated or minority societies, taking advantage of their social components while adding to their minimization.

2.4 Craving for Tasteful or Pattern

At times, social allotment results from a craving for a specific stylish or pattern. Components from different societies are acquired basically on the grounds that they are chic or outwardly engaging, without respect for their social importance.

3. Social Assignment and Personality Misfortune

3.1 Lessening Social Importance

At the point when social components are appropriated without understanding or regard, their social importance can be lessened or minimized. This can prompt a deficiency of importance for the way of life from which they began.

3.2 Disintegration of Social Personality

Rehashed occurrences of social allocation can add to the disintegration of social character. At the point when parts of a culture are acquired and deprived of their specific circumstance, it can sabotage the feeling of character and having a place of the starting local area.

3.3 Support of Generalizations

Social appointment can build up destructive generalizations about the way of life being appropriated. These generalizations propagate misinterpretations and add to the trashing of minimized networks.

3.4 Propagation of Imbalance

Social allotment frequently happens inside the more extensive setting of foundational imbalance and separation. At the point when predominant societies suitable from minimized ones, it can sustain existing power irregular characteristics and add to social deletion.

4. Discussions and Discussions

4.1 Opportunity of Articulation

One of the primary discussions encompassing social apportionment rotates around the standard of opportunity of articulation. Some contend that creative articulation ought not be confined, while others battle that opportunity of articulation ought to be offset with deference for social responsiveness.

4.2 Social Trade versus Appointment

Recognizing social trade and appointment is a disputed matter. Some contend that this differentiation can be trying to make, while others underscore the significance of assent and figuring out in social connections.

4.3 Social Sharing versus Robbery

The line between social sharing and social robbery is frequently obscured. Pundits of social appointment contend that it is a type of burglary, while others battle that social trade is a characteristic piece of human cooperation.

4.4 Job of Purpose

The goal behind social apportionment is a disagreeable issue. A few contend that goal matters and that certified appreciation and understanding can relieve hurt, while others declare that effect is more critical than aim.

5. Instances of Social Allotment

5.1 Local American Crowns

The allotment of Local American hats as style extras is a noticeable model. These hallowed images are frequently worn without grasping their social importance, prompting debate and analysis.

5.2 African Haircuts

African hairdos, for example, cornrows and dreadlocks, have been appropriated by non-African societies without affirmation of their beginnings. This has prompted banters about social heartlessness and irreverence.

5.3 Yoga and Profound Practices

The Western commercialization of yoga and profound practices from South Asia, frequently separated from their otherworldly setting, has raised worries about social assignment and commodification.

5.4 Native Craftsmanship and Images

Native craftsmanship and images have been utilized in style and business items without consent or comprehension of their social importance, prompting allegations of social robbery.

6. Tending to Social Assignment and Character Misfortune

6.1 Instruction and Mindfulness

Training and mindfulness are basic in tending to social allotment. Advancing social getting it, history, and setting can assist people and networks with valuing social variety and keep away from allocation.

6.2 Discourse and Cooperation

Open and conscious discourse between societies can cultivate co-operation and common enhancement. Taking part in social trade with assent and understanding can prompt positive collaborations.

6.3 Affirmation and Attribution

Recognizing the beginning of social components and giving legitimate attribution while getting from different societies is an essential move toward regarding their importance.

6.4 Strengthening and Portrayal

Enabling minimized networks to address and share their way of life legitimately can balance social allocation and advance a more impartial social scene.

7.2 Income Inequality and Economic Disparities

Pay imbalance and monetary variations are basic issues that stand out as of late. These differences address a distinct division between the people who approach riches, assets, and open doors and the individuals who don't. This paper investigates the diverse elements of pay imbalance and monetary inconsistencies, digging into their causes, outcomes, and expected arrangements.

1. Grasping Pay Imbalance and Financial Differences

1.1 Pay Disparity

Pay disparity alludes to the inconsistent conveyance of pay inside a populace. It is normally estimated by markers, for example, the Gini coefficient, which measures the pay conveyance in a general public. A higher Gini coefficient shows more prominent pay disparity.

1.2 Monetary Abberations

Monetary incongruities envelop a more extensive scope of imbalances past pay. They remember variations for riches, admittance to training, medical services, lodging, and

work potential open doors. Financial inconsistencies frequently manifest as a perplexing transaction of variables past pay.

2. **Reasons for Money Imbalance and Monetary Variations**
   2.1 Primary Elements
   Underlying variables, like financial frameworks, strategies, and establishments, assume a huge part in sustaining pay disparity. These variables incorporate expense arrangements, work market elements, and admittance to instruction and medical care.
   2.2 Mechanical Headways
   Mechanical headways, while driving financial development, can compound pay disparity by leaning toward gifted laborers over those with less schooling or concentrated abilities.
   2.3 Globalization
   Globalization has worked with the development of products, administrations, and capital across borders, however it can likewise prompt pay stagnation and occupation dislodging for specific sections of the labor force.
   2.4 Social Elements
   Social elements, for example, segregation in view of race, orientation, or identity, add to financial abberations. Segregation in recruiting, pay, and admittance to assets can propagate disparity.
3. **Outcomes of Pay Imbalance and Monetary Abberations**
   3.1 Social Turmoil
   Elevated degrees of pay imbalance can prompt social agitation and shakiness. At the point when a huge part of the populace feels rejected from financial open doors, it can prompt fights, showings, and even viciousness.
   3.2 Wellbeing Incongruities
   Monetary inconsistencies are firmly connected to wellbeing incongruities. People with lower wages frequently have less admittance to medical services, prompting abberations in wellbeing results, future, and in general prosperity.
   3.3 Instructive Imbalance
   Monetary differences can bring about inconsistent admittance to quality schooling. This sustains patterns of destitution, as people

from impeded foundations frequently face restricted instructive and vocation possibilities.

3.4 Political Impact

Pay imbalance can convert into political impact variations, as those with more prominent abundance have more assets to shape arrangements that benefit their inclinations, possibly misshaping majority rule processes.

4. Worldwide Monetary Variations

4.1 North-South Gap

The worldwide North-South split features variations in monetary improvement among industrialized and non-industrial nations. Many emerging countries battle with neediness, absence of admittance to fundamental administrations, and restricted monetary open doors.

4.2 Abundance Disparity

Abundance disparity is a worldwide worry, with a little level of the total populace holding a critical part of worldwide riches. Expense shelters and seaward records worsen this issue.

4.3 Exchange Irregular characteristics

Exchange irregular characteristics between nations can add to worldwide financial incongruities. A few countries send out labor and products to the detriment of others, sustaining financial imbalance.

4.4 Obligation Weight

Many agricultural nations are troubled with elevated degrees of outside obligation, which restricts their capacity to put resources into monetary turn of events and neediness decrease.

5. Tending to Pay Imbalance and Financial Incongruities

5.1 Moderate Tax assessment

Moderate tax collection, where higher pay workers pay a more prominent level of their pay in charges, can reallocate riches and lessen pay imbalance.

5.2 Instruction and Abilities Improvement

Putting resources into schooling and abilities advancement projects can assist people with obtaining the instruments expected to get to more readily open positions and further develop their financial prosperity.

5.3 Admittance to Medical care

Further developing admittance to medical care administrations, including safeguard care, can lessen wellbeing variations and work on generally prosperity, especially for underestimated networks.

5.4 Social Security Nets

Carrying out friendly security nets, for example, joblessness benefits, food help, and reasonable lodging programs, can give a wellbeing net to people confronting monetary difficulties.

6. **Worldwide Endeavors to Address Financial Inconsistencies**

6.1 Economical Advancement Objectives (SDGs)

The Unified Countries' Manageable Advancement Objectives incorporate focuses to diminish monetary incongruities, further develop admittance to instruction, and kill destitution on a worldwide scale.

6.2 Unfamiliar Guide and Advancement Help

Many created nations give unfamiliar guide and advancement help to address worldwide monetary variations by supporting framework improvement, medical care, training, and neediness lightening programs in agricultural countries.

6.3 Fair Exchange and Moral Industrialism

The fair exchange development advances moral commercialization by guaranteeing that makers in agricultural nations get fair wages and impartial treatment for their items.

6.4 Obligation Help Drive

Obligation help drives plan to lighten the obligation weight of emerging nations, permitting them to divert assets towards financial turn of events and neediness decrease.

7.3 Technological Dependence and Privacy Concerns

In the present interconnected world, innovation has turned into a basic piece of our regular routines. We depend on it for correspondence, data access, amusement, and endless different parts of our reality. While mechanical headways have without a doubt achieved various advantages, they have likewise led to worries about our rising reliance on innovation and the disintegration of protection. This paper investigates the complicated interaction between mechanical reliance and security concerns, analyzing the causes, outcomes, and possible answers for this developing problem.

1. The Ascent of Innovative Reliance

1.1 Pervasive Availability

The multiplication of cell phones, fast web, and interconnected gadgets has made a universe of pervasive network. Individuals can get to data, impart, and perform errands from practically any-place, empowering more noteworthy productivity and accommodation.

1.2 Computerized Change

Enterprises, organizations, and states are going through computerized changes to smooth out activities and improve administrations. This shift has sped up innovative reliance as associations depend on information driven direction and computerization.

1.3 Reliance on Internet based Administrations

Purchasers progressively depend on web-based administrations for shopping, banking, medical care, and amusement. The comfort of these administrations has prompted a reliance on computerized stages.

1.4 Coordination of Brilliant Gadgets

Shrewd gadgets, including voice partners, savvy machines, and wearable innovation, have become indispensable to numerous families. They offer accommodation and productivity yet in addition gather immense measures of individual information.

2. Security Worries in the Advanced Age

2.1 Information Assortment and Observation

The broad assortment of individual information by innovation organizations and states has raised worries about observation and the potential for misuse. Information breaks and holes can bring about the openness of touchy data.

2.2 Algorithmic Inclination

AI calculations, frequently utilized in dynamic cycles, can show predispositions in light of the information they are prepared on. This can sustain separation and imbalance.

2.3 Intrusion of Individual Space

Steady availability through cell phones and web-based entertainment can obscure the limits among public and confidential life, prompting an attack of individual space and limits.

2.4 Dangers to Network safety

The computerized age has achieved a multiplication of cyberattacks, including ransomware, phishing, and hacking. These dangers can think twice about protection and information security.

3. Results of Innovative Reliance and Protection Concerns

3.1 Disintegration of Individual Protection

The assortment and investigation of individual information for different purposes, including designated publicizing and observation, disintegrate individual security. This can have significant mental and cultural ramifications.

3.2 Control and Impact

Innovative stages have the ability to control client conduct and impact sentiments through algorithmic proposals and content curation, possibly subverting majority rule processes.

3.3 Loss of Independence

Reliance on innovation can prompt a deficiency of individual independence. Individuals might feel a sense of urgency to utilize specific gadgets or stages, regardless of whether they have worries about protection or information security.

3.4 Weakness to Cyberattacks

Expanding mechanical reliance makes people and associations more defenseless against cyberattacks. Information breaks and online robbery can bring about monetary misfortunes and individual difficulties.

4. Offsetting Mechanical Progressions with Security Insurance

4.1 Solid Information Security Regulations

Carrying out and implementing solid information security regulations, like the European Association's Overall Information Assurance Guideline (GDPR), can protect people's freedoms to protection and command over their information.

4.2 Protection by Plan

Protection by plan standards ought to be coordinated into the improvement of innovation and computerized administrations all along. This includes considering security suggestions during the plan and execution stages.

4.3 Straightforwardness and Responsibility

Innovation organizations ought to be straightforward about their information assortment and use practices, and they ought to be considered responsible for any abuse or breaks of client information.

4.4 Network safety Measures

Vigorous network safety measures, including encryption, multifaceted verification, and standard security reviews, can assist with safeguarding people and associations from digital dangers.

5. Exploring the Eventual fate of Innovation and Security

5.1 Advanced Education

Advancing computerized education and protection mindfulness is fundamental for people to settle on informed conclusions about their internet based exercises and the dangers related with mechanical reliance.

5.2 Moral Mechanical Turn of events

Tech organizations and designers should focus on moral contemplations, including client protection and information security, all through the turn of events and sending of new advancements.

5.3 Public Discussion and Guideline

People in general ought to participate in banters about the moral and cultural ramifications of innovation, and policymakers ought to sanction guidelines that work out some kind of harmony between mechanical advancement and security assurance.

5.4 Decentralized and Secure Advances

The turn of events and reception of decentralized and secure advancements, for example, blockchain and start to finish encryption, can furnish people with more prominent command over their information and protection.

7.4Environmental Impact of Sashetization

"Sachetization" alludes to the pattern of bundling buyer merchandise in little, single-use sachets or parcels. This approach has become progressively famous, particularly in arising economies, because of its reasonableness and openness. While sachets enjoy their benefits, for example, lessening the forthright expense for shoppers, they additionally accompany huge natural outcomes. This paper investigates the ecological effect of sachetization, featuring the difficulties it presents regarding waste age, asset exhaustion, and biological system interruption.

1. **The Ascent of Sachetization**
   ### 1.1 Reasonable Access
   Sachets give reasonable admittance to a great many items, from individual consideration things like cleanser and cleanser to food fixings, making them open to bring down pay customers.
   ### 1.2 Comfort
   Sachets are minimized and helpful, especially in districts with restricted extra room or where individuals need to buy products in little amounts.
   ### 1.3 Showcasing System

Sachetization is much of the time utilized as a showcasing methodology by organizations to acquaint their items with new business sectors and rival laid out brands.

1.4 Arising Economies

Sachetization has acquired critical notoriety in arising economies, where the expense and openness of items can be huge boundaries to customer reception.

2. Ecological Effect

2.1 Plastic Contamination

The most unmistakable natural issue related with sachetization is plastic contamination. Sachets are regularly produced using single-utilize plastic, which can continue in the climate for many years.

2.2 Waste Age

Sachets add to expanded squander age because of their dispensable nature. Ill-advised removal can prompt littering and the stopping up of waste frameworks, fueling flooding in certain areas.

2.3 Asset Exhaustion

The development of single-use sachets requires critical assets, including non-renewable energy sources for plastic creation and water for assembling and printing processes.

2.4 Biological system Interruption

Ill-advised removal of sachets, particularly in oceanic conditions, can upset biological systems and mischief untamed life. Marine creatures can ingest or become caught in plastic waste.

3. The Sachetization Mystery

3.1 Momentary Advantages versus Long haul Outcomes

Sachetization offers momentary advantages like reasonableness and comfort, yet these benefits frequently come to the detriment of long haul natural outcomes.

3.2 Monetary Expenses of Cleanup

The financial expenses of tidying up plastic contamination brought about by sachetization, including endeavors to eliminate litter and moderate ecological harm, can offset the underlying monetary advantages of reasonableness.

3.3 Wellbeing Suggestions

Plastic contamination coming about because of sachetization can have antagonistic wellbeing suggestions for people and untamed life, as poisons from plastic waste can enter the pecking order.

3.4 Other options and Manageable Arrangements

There is a need to investigate choices and reasonable arrangements that offset moderateness and comfort with natural obligation.

4. Arrangements and Moderation Systems

4.1 Advancement of Reusing

Endeavors to advance reusing and legitimate waste administration are vital in alleviating the ecological effect of sachetization. Executing compelling reusing programs and working on squander assortment and removal foundation can assist with lessening plastic contamination.

4.2 Biodegradable Bundling

Organizations can investigate biodegradable or compostable bundling materials as an option in contrast to conventional single-utilize plastic sachets. These materials separate all the more rapidly and are less destructive to the climate.

4.3 Broadened Maker Obligation (EPR)

Carrying out broadened maker obligation projects can consider makers responsible for the finish of-life the executives of their items. This urges organizations to plan items in light of natural contemplations and assume a sense of ownership with their legitimate removal.

4.4 Buyer Schooling

Teaching buyers about the ecological results of sachetization and advancing feasible utilization propensities can prompt better waste administration and a decrease in single-utilize plastic utilization.

5. Contextual analyses

5.1 India: The Sachet Economy

India has seen critical development in the sachet economy, with items going from cleanser to flavors bundled in little, reasonable sachets. While these sachets give openness, they have added to plastic contamination and natural debasement. India is currently investigating choices, including empowering the utilization of top off stations for normal family items.

5.2 The Philippines: Without sachet Drive

The Philippines has sent off the "Without sachet" drive to diminish single-use sachet squander. Organizations are urged to take on more reasonable bundling choices and participate in reusing and squander the board endeavors.

8

Chapter8

Opportunities and Solutions

In a world described by quick change and steady development, valuable open doors and arrangements arise as fundamental features of our aggregate process. Whether we are tending to worldwide difficulties, cultivating development, or taking a stab at self-improvement, valuable open doors and arrangements are the main impetuses that push us forward. In this complete investigation, we will dig into different open doors and arrangements that range across assorted fields, giving experiences into how they shape our reality and empower us to defeat complex difficulties.

1. **Open doors for Advancement**
   1.1 Mechanical Headways
   The quick speed of mechanical headways gives various open doors to advancement across different areas. Arising advances like man-made reasoning, biotechnology, and environmentally friendly power open ways to groundbreaking arrangements in medical care, agribusiness, and maintainability.
   1.2 Advanced Change
   The advanced change of enterprises offers valuable chances to

streamline processes, improve client encounters, and foster new plans of action. Web based business, remote work, and computerized diversion are only a couple of instances of regions where development flourishes.

1.3 Feasible Turn of events

The worldwide shift toward feasible advancement presents potential open doors for organizations and people to adjust their endeavors to natural and social obligation. Developments in efficient power energy, roundabout economies, and eco-accommodating items make ready for a more reasonable future.

1.4 Space Investigation

Headways in space investigation innovation are setting out open doors for logical revelation, asset investigation, and, surprisingly, likely colonization of different planets. The commercialization of room guarantees new businesses and financial development.

2. Answers for Worldwide Difficulties

2.1 Environmental Change Alleviation

Tending to environmental change is perhaps of the most squeezing worldwide test. Arrangements incorporate progressing to environmentally friendly power sources, reforestation, carbon catch innovations, and global participation through arrangements like the Paris Understanding.

2.2 General Wellbeing

The Coronavirus pandemic highlighted the significance of worldwide general wellbeing arrangements. Methodologies incorporate immunization conveyance, pandemic readiness, and fortifying medical services frameworks around the world.

2.3 Neediness Lightening

Endeavors to mitigate destitution include a blend of monetary turn of events, social wellbeing nets, schooling, and microfinance drives. Imaginative arrangements like contingent money moves and social effect effective money management plan to inspire minimized networks.

2.4 Schooling Access

Growing admittance to quality schooling is essential for worldwide turn of events. Arrangements incorporate internet learning stages, grants for oppressed understudies, and instructor preparing projects to work on instructive results.

3. Financial Open doors and Arrangements

3.1 Business

Business offers people the chance to enhance, make occupations, and drive monetary development. Support for new businesses, admittance to capital, and cultivating pioneering environments can fuel monetary turn of events.

3.2 Monetary Incorporation

Offering monetary types of assistance to the unbanked and underbanked populaces presents a financial open door. Arrangements incorporate portable banking, microfinance foundations, and computerized installment frameworks.

3.3 Exchange and Globalization

Worldwide exchange and globalization can help economies by extending markets, making position, and advancing monetary association. International alliances and framework improvement work with worldwide monetary open doors.

3.4 Monetary Versatility

Building monetary versatility includes enhancing enterprises, putting resources into innovative work, and making wellbeing nets to endure financial shocks, like downturns or catastrophic events.

4. Ecological Protection and Manageability

4.1 Environmentally friendly power Progress

Progressing to environmentally friendly power sources like sun based, wind, and hydropower is an answer for battle environmental change and diminish fossil fuel byproducts. This shift presents open doors for green positions and clean energy enterprises.

4.2 Protection and Biodiversity

Preservation endeavors expect to safeguard environments, protect biodiversity, and battle territory misfortune. Open doors incorporate maintainable farming practices, untamed life the travel industry, and rewilding drives.

4.3 Roundabout Economy

The reception of a roundabout economy model, where items are intended for life span and reusing, decreases waste and moderates assets. Organizations can profit from diminished costs and expanded supportability.

4.4 Manageable Farming

Developments in supportable agribusiness, for example, accuracy cultivating and natural practices, advance food security while limiting ecological effect.

5. Wellbeing and Prosperity

5.1 Telehealth and Remote Medication

Telehealth arrangements give admittance to medical care benefits from a distance, connecting geological holes and further developing medical care openness.

5.2 Psychological well-being Mindfulness

Expanded consciousness of emotional well-being issues has prompted the improvement of psychological wellness administrations, encouraging groups of people, and destigmatization endeavors.

5.3 All encompassing Prosperity

All encompassing prosperity approaches center around physical, mental, and profound wellbeing. Potential open doors incorporate wellbeing programs, care rehearses, and comprehensive medical care administrations.

5.4 Medical care Development

Developments in medical care, for example, accuracy medication, quality treatment, and clinical innovation progressions, give new answers for treating and forestalling sicknesses.

6. Schooling and Deep rooted Learning

6.1 Deep rooted Learning Potential open doors

Long lasting learning valuable open doors permit people to procure new abilities, remain pertinent in the gig market, and seek after self-improvement all through their lives.

6.2 Internet based Schooling

Online schooling stages offer available and adaptable learning open doors, taking care of assorted needs and socioeconomics.

6.3 Upskilling and Reskilling

Upskilling and reskilling programs assist people with progressing to new vocations or adjust to changing position prerequisites.

6.4 Instructive Access for All

Endeavors to give instructive admittance to minimized populaces, including displaced people and underserved networks, advance fairness and worldwide turn of events.

7. Self-improvement and Personal growth

7.1 Objective Setting and Accomplishment

Laying out private and expert objectives cultivates personal development, inspiration, and a feeling of achievement.

7.2 Care and Prosperity Practices

Care, reflection, and prosperity rehearses add to mental and close to home prosperity, improving self-awareness.

7.3 Self-Reflection and Versatility

Self-reflection and versatility are fundamental for self-improvement, empowering people to gain from encounters and adjust to new difficulties.

7.4 Local area Commitment

Drawing in with networks and social drives gives amazing open doors to self-improvement through joint effort and effect.

8.1Promoting Cultural Exchange and Understanding

In our undeniably interconnected world, advancing social trade and understanding has become vital for encouraging worldwide congruity and collaboration. Social trade includes the sharing of thoughts, customs, customs, and encounters among people and gatherings from various social foundations. This improving system helps separate generalizations, fabricate compassion, and fortify the securities that interface us as people. In this paper, we will investigate the significance of social trade and understanding, the advantages it brings, and how it tends to be advanced on an individual, cultural, and worldwide level.

1. **The Meaning of Social Trade**
   1.1. Empowering Discourse
   Social trade supports open and significant exchange between individuals from various societies. It gives a stage to people to share their accounts, convictions, and encounters, cultivating common regard and understanding.
   1.2. Encouraging Compassion
   Drawing in with different societies permits people to step into the shoes of others, creating sympathy for individuals with various foundations, convictions, and viewpoints.
   1.3. Separating Generalizations
   Social trade scatters generalizations and misinterpretations by offering firsthand encounters and communications that challenge assumptions.
   1.4. Safeguarding Social Legacy
   Through social trade, customs, dialects, and works of art are saved and shared, forestalling their disintegration and adding to social variety.
2. **Advantages of Social Trade**
   2.1. Upgrading Worldwide Citizenship
   Social trade encourages a feeling of worldwide citizenship by advancing resilience, regard for variety, and a common obligation regarding the world's difficulties.
   2.2. Propelling Harmony and Strategy
   Social trade assumes a part in strategy and compromise,

permitting countries to construct scaffolds and resolve contrasts through social tact.

2.3. Helping The travel industry and Economy

Social trade animates the travel industry and financial development by drawing in guests keen on encountering neighborhood societies, customs, and foods.

2.4. Propelling Training

Social trade programs in schools and colleges give understudies important global openness, language abilities, and diverse capability.

3. Advancing Social Trade on an Individual Level

3.1. Travel and Investigation

Making a trip to various nations and locales is one of the most immediate methods for participating in social trade. It permits people to drench themselves in new societies, attempt new food varieties, and draw in with local people.

3.2. Learning Another Dialect

Learning another dialect opens ways to understanding and associating with individuals from various societies. Language abilities can work with more profound discussions and social appreciation.

3.3. Social Drenching

Living and working abroad or in different networks considers social drenching, encouraging a more profound comprehension of nearby traditions and customs.

3.4. Taking part in Comprehensive developments

Taking part in comprehensive developments, celebrations, and festivities in one's own local area or abroad gives chances to find out about and value different societies.

4. Cultural and Hierarchical Drives

4.1. Social Trade Projects

Instructive establishments, NGOs, and states can advance social trade programs that work with understudy trades, temporary jobs, and social drenching encounters.

4.2. Social Celebrations

Coordinating social celebrations and occasions that exhibit various customs and fine arts can unite networks and advance culturally diverse comprehension.

4.3. Multicultural Instruction

Integrating multicultural instruction into school educational plans urges understudies to find out about and value assorted societies since the beginning.

4.4. Social Strategy

States and worldwide associations can take part in social strategy, involving social trades as devices for global collaboration and peacebuilding.

5. Global Drives and Tact

5.1. Social Trade Arrangements

Nations can consent to respective or multilateral arrangements to advance social trade, permitting craftsmen, researchers, and residents to traverse borders.

5.2. UNESCO's Job

UNESCO (Joined Countries Instructive, Logical and Social Association) assumes a crucial part in defending social legacy and advancing social trade through different drives and projects.

5.3. Culturally diverse Organizations

Worldwide associations, NGOs, and organizations can shape culturally diverse organizations to cultivate trade and grasping on a worldwide scale.

5.4. Advancing Social Negotiators

Countries can delegate social negotiators and representatives to advance their way of life and encourage generosity in different nations.

6. Challenges and Conquering Obstructions

6.1. Generalizations and Biases

Generalizations and biases can obstruct social trade. Beating these obstructions requires training, exchange, and openness to assorted viewpoints.

6.2. Language Obstructions

Language contrasts can present difficulties to correspondence. Language-learning drives and interpretation apparatuses can assist with overcoming this issue.

6.3. Political and Financial Boundaries

Political pressures and monetary incongruities can influence social trade. Discretion, global participation, and financing can resolve these issues.

6.4. Social Awareness

Regarding social responsive qualities and practices is critical for effective trade. Schooling and mindfulness building can assist members with exploring social contrasts deferentially.

8.2 Sustainable Sashetization Practices

Sachetization, the act of bundling buyer merchandise in little, single-use sachets or parcels, has acquired notoriety because of its moderateness and comfort, especially in arising economies. In any case, the far reaching utilization of single-use sachets has raised worries about their natural effect, considering that they are frequently made of non-biodegradable materials. To address these worries, fundamental to investigate maintainable sachetization rehearses balance the comfort of little bundling with ecological obligation. This exposition digs into economical sachetization works on, featuring their significance, advantages, difficulties, and possible arrangements.

1. The Meaning of Practical Sachetization

1.1. Ecological Worries

Customary sachetization, which depends on single-utilize plastic bundling, contributes fundamentally to plastic contamination, prompting litter, natural surroundings debasement, and damage to untamed life.

1.2. Asset Proficiency

Supportable sachetization means to streamline asset use by decreasing the materials expected for bundling, limiting energy utilization during creation, and bringing transportation costs due down to lightweight bundling.

1.3. Customer Mindfulness

As ecological mindfulness among buyers develops, there is an interest for items that line up with manageability values. Maintainable sachetization can satisfy this need and upgrade brand notoriety.

1.4. Administrative Tensions

Unofficial laws and approaches pointed toward diminishing plastic waste and advancing feasible practices are pushing organizations to take on more eco-accommodating sachetization strategies.

2. Economical Sachetization Practices

2.1. Biodegradable Materials

Supplanting customary plastic sachets with biodegradable materials, for example, plant-based plastics (bioplastics) or paper, is a reasonable other option. These materials separate all the more quickly in the climate, lessening their environmental impression.

2.2. Eco-Accommodating Inks and Printing

Utilizing eco-accommodating inks and printing techniques on sachet bundling can limit the natural effect of marking and marking while at the same time keeping up with item data.

2.3. Refillable Sachets

Acquainting refillable sachets empowers clients with reuse their bundling by buying tops off, diminishing waste and moderating assets.

2.4. Lightweight Plan

Advancing sachet plan to diminish how much material expected while keeping up with item trustworthiness can improve supportability without compromising comfort.

3. **Advantages of Economical Sachetization**

3.1. Diminished Plastic Contamination

Supportable sachetization limits the utilization of single-use plastics, which are a significant supporter of plastic contamination in seas and environments.

3.2. Lower Carbon Impression

Lightweight, eco-accommodating materials and manageable creation rehearses add to bring down energy utilization and ozone depleting substance emanations during sachet creation and transportation.

3.3. Positive Brand Picture

Organizations taking on economical sachetization practices can upgrade their image picture by showing obligation to ecological obligation.

3.4. Market Intensity

As supportability turns into a focal thought for customers, organizations carrying out feasible sachetization rehearses gain an upper hand on the lookout.

4. **Difficulties and Arrangements**

4.1. Cost Contemplations

The underlying expense of changing to manageable sachetization practices can be higher because of interests in new materials and creation processes. Notwithstanding, long haul cost reserve funds can balance these underlying costs.

4.2. Buyer Conduct

Instructing customers about the advantages of practical sachetization and changing buying propensities to lean toward eco-accommodating choices can be a test. Organizations can address this through promoting efforts and motivators.

4.3. Production network Intricacy

Presenting supportable sachetization might require changes in the store network, including obtaining of materials, creation cycles, and conveyance strategies. Cooperative endeavors with providers and accomplices can facilitate this change.

4.4. Adaptability

Increasing maintainable sachetization practices to satisfy the needs of bigger business sectors or worldwide development might present difficulties, requiring vital preparation and ventures.

5. Contextual investigations

5.1. Unilever's Supportable Sachets

Unilever, a worldwide customer products organization, has been effectively addressing natural worries connected with sachetization. They have presented sachets produced using reused plastics and have laid out assortment and reusing projects to advance practical sachet use.

5.2. Reusable Sachets in Southeast Asia

In a few Southeast Asian nations, refillable sachets have acquired prevalence. Buyers buy the underlying item in a strong sachet and afterward top off it at lower cost, decreasing single-use sachet squander.

8.3 Ethical Globalization Initiatives

Globalization, the course of expanded interconnectedness and relationship among nations and districts, has brought the two open doors and difficulties. While it has energized financial development and mechanical progressions, it has likewise prompted social, monetary, and ecological abberations. Moral globalization drives look to address these difficulties by advancing decency, supportability, and inclusivity in the globalized world. In this article, we will investigate the meaning of moral globalization, look at different drives, and talk about their effects on worldwide social orders and economies.

1. The Meaning of Moral Globalization
1.1. Tending to Worldwide Disparities

Moral globalization drives plan to address worldwide disparities in exchange, abundance conveyance, and admittance to assets by advancing a more fair dissemination of advantages.

1.2. Natural Supportability

Maintainability is a focal topic in moral globalization, underlining capable asset the board, environment activity, and the security of biological systems.

1.3. Civil rights

Advancing civil rights is a center part of moral globalization, with an emphasis on common freedoms, fair work practices, and orientation uniformity.

1.4. Inclusivity and Variety

Moral globalization looks to guarantee that the advantages of globalization are shared by assorted populaces, including under-estimated networks and native people groups.

2. Key Moral Globalization Drives

2.1. Fair Exchange Development

The fair exchange development centers around making impartial exchanging connections between makers agricultural nations and purchasers in the created world. It guarantees fair wages, moral work rehearses, and supportable cultivating strategies.

2.2. Corporate Social Obligation (CSR)

CSR drives urge organizations to coordinate moral and social contemplations into their business techniques. This incorporates mindful obtaining, ecological stewardship, and charitable endeavors.

2.3. Joined Countries Maintainable Improvement Objectives (SDGs)

The Unified Countries has set 17 SDGs to address worldwide difficulties, including neediness, disparity, environmental change, and admittance to clean water and sterilization. These objectives act as a system for moral globalization.

2.4. The Worldwide Conservative

The UN Worldwide Conservative urges organizations and associations to take on feasible and socially dependable arrangements. Signatories focus on ten standards connected with common liberties, work, the climate, and hostile to debasement.

3. Effects of Moral Globalization Drives

3.1. Financial Development with Value

Moral globalization drives add to financial development while guaranteeing that the advantages are circulated all the more evenhandedly among laborers, little makers, and underestimated networks.

3.2. Destitution Decrease

Through fair exchange rehearses and dependable obtaining, moral globalization drives assist with lifting individuals out of destitution by giving fair wages and stable vocations.

3.3. Natural Stewardship

Maintainability endeavors inside moral globalization add to ecological security, preservation of regular assets, and the decrease of ozone harming substance outflows.

3.4. Further developed Work Conditions

CSR drives and fair exchange rehearses advance respectable work conditions, including fair wages, safe working environments, and the end of youngster and constrained work.

4. Difficulties and Reactions

4.1. Authorization and Responsibility

Implementing moral guidelines and considering associations responsible for their activities can be testing, particularly in worldwide stockpile chains where straightforwardness might need.

4.2. Monetary Interests

Some contend that moral globalization drives can be seen as restricting financial development and rivalry, as sticking to moral guidelines might inflate costs for organizations.

4.3. Social Awareness

Applying worldwide moral guidelines across different societies and social orders can challenge, as standards and values shift generally across areas.

4.4. Holes in Execution

There are holes in the execution of moral globalization drives, for certain organizations or locales lingering behind in taking on mindful practices.

5. Contextual investigations

5.1. Fair Exchange Espresso

The fair exchange espresso development has changed the espresso business by guaranteeing that limited scale espresso makers get fair remuneration for their items. This drive has worked on the jobs of millions of espresso ranchers around the world.

5.2. The UN Worldwide Reduced and Business Maintainability

Various organizations, including large companies, have marked the UN Worldwide Reduced, focusing on moral and maintainable strategic approaches. These organizations have taken critical steps in decreasing their natural impression and advancing social obligation.

6. Future Headings and End

6.1. Fortifying Moral Structures

Future moral globalization drives should zero in on fortifying worldwide moral structures, upgrading responsibility systems, and expanding straightforwardness in supply chains.

6.2. Inclusivity and Strengthening

Endeavors ought to be made to guarantee that minimized networks, native people groups, and ladies are effectively engaged with molding moral globalization drives and profiting from them.

6.3. Economical Turn of events

The UN SDGs give a thorough guide to moral globalization. Progress toward these objectives ought to keep on being a focal point of worldwide endeavors.

6.4. Worldwide Cooperation

Tending to worldwide difficulties requires coordinated effort among state run administrations, organizations, common society, and people. Moral globalization drives give a stage to such coordinated effort.

8.4 Policy Recommendations

In a quickly impacting world, compelling strategies assume a basic part in shaping social orders, economies, and conditions. Strategy suggestions are the main thrust behind informed decision-production by states, associations, and people. This exposition dives into key strategy suggestions across different areas, stressing the significance of proof based, ground breaking ways to deal with address complex difficulties and advance practical and comprehensive development.

1. **Monetary Arrangement Suggestions**

   1.1. Pay Rearrangement

   Execute moderate duty approaches that reallocate riches, decrease pay disparity, and give social security nets to safeguard weak populaces.

   1.2. Interest in Schooling and Abilities

   Cultivate monetary development by putting resources into schooling and abilities improvement programs, guaranteeing that the labor force stays versatile and serious in the worldwide economy.

   1.3. Feasible Monetary Practices

   Advance feasible monetary practices that think about ecological and social effects. Empower round economies, green ventures, and mindful asset the board.

   1.4. Development and Business

   Support advancement and business through innovative work motivators, admittance to investment, and smoothed out guidelines to prod monetary development and occupation creation.

2. **Ecological Strategy Proposals**

   2.1. Environment Activity

   Carry out extensive environment activity approaches, including carbon valuing, sustainable power motivating forces, and emanations decrease focuses, to relieve the effects of environmental change.

2.2. Preservation and Biodiversity

Safeguard biodiversity and biological systems through safeguarded regions, maintainable land use arranging, and impetuses for mindful asset the board.

2.3. Contamination Control

Authorize severe contamination control guidelines, advance clean innovations, and urge businesses to embrace eco-accommodating practices to diminish contamination and safeguard air and water quality.

2.4. Round Economy Change

Support the progress to a roundabout economy by boosting reusing, diminishing waste, and advancing practical item plan and assembling.

3. Social Strategy Proposals

3.1. General Medical services

Guarantee admittance to reasonable and quality medical services through widespread medical services frameworks that cover all residents, advancing wellbeing value and lessening medical care incongruities.

3.2. Schooling Access

Grow admittance to quality schooling at all levels, especially for minimized networks, by putting resources into foundation, educator preparing, and innovation.

3.3. Orientation Equity

Advance orientation equity through approaches that address orientation based savagery, close the orientation pay hole, and increment ladies' portrayal in positions of authority.

3.4. Social Wellbeing Nets

Lay out strong social wellbeing nets, including joblessness benefits and reasonable lodging programs, to safeguard weak populaces during financial slumps.

4. Innovation and Computerized Arrangement Suggestions

4.1. Computerized Protection and Security

Authorize severe guidelines on information security and network safety, guaranteeing people's freedoms are safeguarded in the advanced age.

4.2. Advanced Consideration

Span the advanced separation by giving reasonable web access, computerized proficiency projects, and innovation endowments to underserved networks.

4.3. Moral computer based intelligence and Robotization

Foster moral rules for man-made consciousness and robotization to guarantee mindful turn of events and organization of these innovations, limiting likely adverse consequences on work and protection.

4.4. Development Environments

Advance development environments through research subsidizing, support for new companies, and organizations between the scholarly community, industry, and government.

5. Worldwide and International strategy Proposals

5.1. Global Collaboration

Fortify worldwide collaboration through collusions and associations to address worldwide difficulties, including environmental change, general wellbeing emergencies, and philanthropic emergencies.

5.2. Philanthropic Guide and Improvement Help

Increment philanthropic guide and improvement help to nations out of luck, zeroing in on neediness decrease, foundation advancement, and medical services access.

5.3. Compromise

Put resources into tact and compromise endeavors to forestall and determine clashes through tranquil means, decreasing worldwide flimsiness and instability.

5.4. Multilateral Arrangements

Support and maintain multilateral arrangements, like the Paris

Understanding and the Unified Countries Manageable Improvement Objectives, to by and large handle worldwide issues.

6. Difficulties and Contemplations

6.1. Execution Difficulties

Some good natured approaches face difficulties during execution, like opposition from partners, financial plan imperatives, and unanticipated outer variables. Legislatures and associations must proactively address these issues.

6.2. Momentary versus Long haul Effect

Adjusting momentary requirements and long haul manageability can be a test. Policymakers should cautiously consider the potential compromises between prompt outcomes and feasible, enduring change.

6.3. Strategy Assessment

Ordinary assessment and change of strategies are fundamental to guarantee their viability. Lay out instruments for progressing appraisal and input from partners.

6.4. Worldwide Coordinated effort

Tending to worldwide difficulties frequently requires cooperation among countries. Policymakers ought to effectively participate in discretionary endeavors and discussions to construct agreement and encourage collaboration

9

Chapter9

Future Trends and Prospects

As we stand on the cusp of another time, the world is seeing extraordinary changes and progressions in different circles of life. What's to come is portrayed by fast mechanical advancement, moving socioeconomics, developing financial ideal models, and worldwide difficulties that request our consideration and resourcefulness. This paper investigates what's in store patterns and prospects that are set to shape our reality in the next few decades, offering bits of knowledge into the difficulties and open doors that lie ahead.

1. Mechanical Headways

1.1. Man-made reasoning and Robotization

The proceeded with improvement of man-made reasoning (simulated intelligence) and robotization innovations is set to change enterprises and work markets. As man-made intelligence turns out to be more complex, it will affect everything from medical services and transportation to back and assembling.

1.2. Quantum Figuring

Quantum processing vows to open new degrees of computational power, possibly changing fields like cryptography, drug disclosure, and environment demonstrating.

1.3. Web of Things (IoT)

The expansion of IoT gadgets will associate regular items to the web, empowering more brilliant urban areas, more productive asset the board, and further developed medical services observing.

1.4. Biotechnology and Genomics

Headways in biotechnology and genomics will prompt customized medication, quality altering, and leap forwards in the treatment of hereditary illnesses.

2. Segment Movements

2.1. Maturing Populaces

Numerous nations are encountering maturing populaces, prompting difficulties in medical care, benefits frameworks, and work markets. Systems to resolve these issues will turn out to be progressively significant.

2.2. Urbanization

Urbanization patterns are supposed to proceed, with additional individuals moving to urban areas. This will require foundation advancement, supportable metropolitan preparation, and answers for address blockage and contamination.

2.3. Movement and Relocation

Worldwide movement examples will advance because of environmental change, struggle, and monetary abberations. Dealing with the effects of relocation and dislodging will be quite difficult for countries and global associations.

2.4. Variety and Consideration

Developing variety in social orders will expect endeavors to advance social union, kill separation, and guarantee equivalent open doors for all.

3. Financial Standards

3.1. Gig Economy and Remote Work

The gig economy and remote work are turning out to be more common, changing conventional business structures. Policymakers should adjust work guidelines and social wellbeing nets appropriately.

3.2. Economical Economies

Maintainability will be a main thrust in monetary turn of events. Organizations and legislatures should focus on ecological obligation, round economies, and clean energy arrangements.

3.3. Computerized Monetary forms

The ascent of computerized monetary forms, including cryptographic forms of money and national bank advanced monetary forms (CBDCs), may reshape monetary frameworks and the manner in which we manage exchanges.

3.4. Worldwide Stock Chains

The Coronavirus pandemic uncovered weaknesses in worldwide stock chains. Future patterns might include reshoring, regionalization, and expansion of supply chains.

4. Worldwide Difficulties

4.1. Environmental Change

Environmental change stays perhaps of the most squeezing worldwide test. Alleviating its belongings through outflows decrease, variation measures, and maintainable practices is urgent.

4.2. General Wellbeing

Worldwide wellbeing dangers, like pandemics, anti-infection opposition, and non-transmittable sicknesses, will require global participation and interest in medical care frameworks.

4.3. Network protection

The computerized age brings new network safety dangers, including cyberattacks on basic framework and information breaks. Reinforcing online protection measures and worldwide participation is basic.

4.4. International Pressures

International pressures between countries, especially extraordinary powers, could affect worldwide dependability, exchange, and global relations. Political endeavors will be urgent in dealing with these strains.

5. Possibilities and Valuable open doors

5.1. Maintainability Arrangements

The change to a maintainable future presents immense open doors in environmentally friendly power, green innovations, reasonable horticulture, and protection endeavors.

5.2. Medical care Advancements

Progressions in medical services, including telemedicine, customized medication, and genomics, offer the potential for worked on understanding results and expanded admittance to mind.

5.3. Schooling Change

The digitalization of schooling can democratize admittance to learning assets and empower long lasting picking up, giving open doors to expertise improvement and professional success.

5.4. Space Investigation

The developing interest in space investigation and business space adventures holds possibilities for logical revelation, asset investigation, and likely answers for Earth's concerns.

6. Difficulties and Concerns

6.1. Moral Issues

As innovation progresses, moral worries encompassing man-made intelligence morals, biotechnology, and security should be addressed to guarantee dependable advancement.

6.2. Financial Differences

While mechanical progressions can set out monetary open doors, they additionally can possibly worsen financial incongruities and occupation removal.

6.3. Ecological Supportability

Tending to environmental change and ecological corruption will require purposeful worldwide endeavors and political will to sanction significant arrangements and drives.

6.4. Worldwide Administration

Fortifying worldwide administration systems will be vital for address transnational difficulties and guarantee participation among countries.

9.1 The Role of AI and Automation

Man-made consciousness (artificial intelligence) and robotization have become crucial drivers of mechanical advancement, changing enterprises, and reshaping the manner in which we live and work. These advancements, controlled by AI calculations, mechanical technology, and information examination, are mechanizing errands, improving dynamic cycles, and changing different areas of the economy. In this paper, we will investigate the complex job of computer based intelligence and robotization, their effect on enterprises, the advantages and difficulties they present, and their suggestions for the eventual fate of work and society.

1. ## The Development of artificial intelligence and Robotization

   ### 1.1. AI and Profound Learning

   The development of simulated intelligence has been set apart by critical progressions in AI and profound learning calculations. These advancements empower PCs to gain from information, perceive examples, and make expectations, making them fundamental apparatuses for robotization.

   ### 1.2. Mechanical technology and Robotization

   Mechanical frameworks outfitted with man-made intelligence capacities have acquired noticeable quality across ventures, computerizing undertakings in assembling, medical services, planned operations, and then some. These robots can perform redundant, risky, and exact errands with effectiveness.

   ### 1.3. Regular Language Handling (NLP)

   NLP methods empower machines to comprehend and produce human language, making ready for applications, for example, chatbots, menial helpers, and language interpretation administrations.

1.4. Independent Vehicles

Artificial intelligence and robotization play had a focal impact in the improvement of independent vehicles, promising more secure and more effective transportation frameworks.

2. Influence on Businesses

2.1. Assembling and Industry 4.0

Computer based intelligence fueled advanced mechanics and robotization have changed assembling processes, prompting Industry 4.0, where shrewd plants streamline creation, lessen personal time, and further develop item quality.

2.2. Medical services and Diagnostics

Man-made intelligence has taken huge steps in medical care, helping with sickness analysis, drug revelation, and customized therapy plans. Robotization in medical services smoothes out regulatory assignments and improves patient consideration.

2.3. Finance and Fintech

In the monetary area, artificial intelligence calculations are utilized for misrepresentation identification, algorithmic exchanging, and credit scoring. Fintech new businesses are utilizing computerization to offer imaginative monetary administrations.

2.4. Agribusiness and Accuracy Cultivating

Computerization in horticulture, combined with man-made intelligence driven accuracy cultivating, improves crop yields, limits asset waste, and upgrades maintainable cultivating rehearses.

2.5. Retail and Client support

Retailers use computer based intelligence for stock administration, request estimating, and customized promoting. Chatbots and menial helpers give robotized client assistance and backing.

3. Advantages of artificial intelligence and Robotization

3.1. Effectiveness and Efficiency

Computer based intelligence and mechanization further develop proficiency by performing undertakings quicker and more precisely than people, prompting expanded efficiency in different ventures.

3.2. Cost Decrease

Robotization decreases work costs, particularly for dreary undertakings, while man-made intelligence can advance asset distribution, prompting cost investment funds.

3.3. Wellbeing and Chance Moderation

In ventures like assembling and medical services, computerization upgrades security by diminishing human mistake. Independent vehicles vow to diminish mishaps out and about.

3.4. Information Driven Navigation

Simulated intelligence examines immense datasets to separate significant bits of knowledge, empowering information driven dynamic that can further develop business methodologies and results.

4. Difficulties and Concerns

4.1. Work Uprooting

The computerization of routine errands raises worries about work uprooting. A few laborers might confront joblessness or the need to procure new abilities.

4.2. Abilities Hole

The quick reception of computer based intelligence and robotization requires a labor force with refreshed abilities. Spanning the abilities hole is a test that requires interests in schooling and preparing.

4.3. Moral Worries

Simulated intelligence calculations can sustain predispositions present in preparing information, prompting biased results. Guaranteeing reasonableness and moral utilization of simulated intelligence is a basic concern.

4.4. Protection and Security

The assortment and examination of tremendous measures of information raise protection and security concerns. Shielding delicate data from breaks and abuse is fundamental.

5. The Eventual fate of Work and Society

5.1. Upskilling and Reskilling

The eventual fate of work will require constant upskilling and reskilling of the labor force to adjust to changing position jobs and necessities.

5.2. Human-computer based intelligence Joint effort

As opposed to supplanting people, computer based intelligence and robotization can expand human capacities, prompting coordinated effort among machines and people in different callings.

5.3. Moral man-made intelligence Improvement

Tending to moral worries in man-made intelligence improvement will be pivotal to guarantee that these advances benefit society in general and don't worsen existing imbalances.

5.4. Administrative Systems

States and associations should lay out administrative systems that administer simulated intelligence and mechanization to guarantee their dependable use and adherence to moral norms.

9.2 Environmental Sustainability in Sachetization

Sachetization, the act of bundling buyer merchandise in little, single-use sachets or parcels, has acquired notoriety for its benefit and reasonableness, especially in arising economies. Be that as it may, the boundless utilization of single-use sachets produced using non-biodegradable materials has raised worries about its natural effect. In this paper, we will investigate the difficulties of natural supportability in sachetization, likely arrangements, and the significance of embracing eco-accommodating bundling practices to alleviate the biological impression of this bundling pattern.

1. The Natural Effect of Sachetization

1.1. Plastic Contamination

Conventional sachetization frequently depends on plastic bundling, which contributes fundamentally to worldwide plastic contamination. Disposed of sachets can wind up in seas and environments, hurting marine life and biological systems.

1.2. Non-Biodegradable Materials

Numerous sachet materials are non-biodegradable, requiring many years to deteriorate. Thus, they collect in landfills and regular habitats.

1.3. Asset Utilization

The creation of single-use sachets requires assets, for example, petrol based plastics and energy, adding to asset exhaustion and ozone depleting substance outflows.

1.4. Absence of Reusing

In numerous districts, sachets are not effectively recyclable because of their little size and material arrangement, prompting low reusing rates.

2. Manageable Sachetization Practices

2.1. Biodegradable Materials

One of the most encouraging answers for ecological maintainability in sachetization is the utilization of biodegradable materials. Bioplastics got from inexhaustible sources, like cornstarch or sugarcane, can supplant customary plastics.

2.2. Eco-Accommodating Inks and Printing

The utilization of eco-accommodating inks and printing techniques on sachet bundling can lessen the natural effect of naming and marking, guaranteeing that these components don't add to contamination.

2.3. Refillable Sachets

Presenting refillable sachets can lessen squander. Shoppers buy the underlying item in a sturdy sachet and afterward buy tops off, limiting the quantity of single-use sachets.

2.4. Lightweight Plan

Streamlining sachet plan to lessen material use while keeping up with item trustworthiness can improve maintainability without compromising accommodation.

3. **The Advantages of Supportable Sachetization**

3.1. Decreased Plastic Contamination

Supportable sachetization limits the utilization of single-use plastics, a significant supporter of plastic contamination in seas and environments.

3.2. Lower Carbon Impression

Lightweight, eco-accommodating materials and reasonable creation rehearses add to bring down energy utilization and ozone harming substance emanations during sachet creation and transportation.

3.3. Positive Brand Picture

Organizations embracing reasonable sachetization practices can improve their image picture by showing a promise to natural obligation.

3.4. Market Intensity

As supportability turns into a focal thought for purchasers, organizations executing feasible sachetization rehearses gain an upper hand on the lookout.

4. **Difficulties and Boundaries**

4.1. Cost Contemplations

The underlying expense of progressing to economical sachetization practices can be higher because of interests in new materials and creation processes. In any case, long haul cost reserve funds can balance these underlying costs.

4.2. Shopper Conduct

Instructing buyers about the advantages of maintainable sachetization and changing buying propensities to incline toward eco-accommodating choices can be a test. Organizations can address this through advertising efforts and impetuses.

4.3. Production network Intricacy

Presenting supportable sachetization might require changes in the store network, including obtaining of materials, creation cycles, and appropriation strategies. Cooperative endeavors with providers and accomplices can facilitate this change.

4.4. Adaptability

Increasing economical sachetization practices to satisfy the needs of bigger business sectors or global extension might present difficulties, requiring key preparation and ventures.

5. Contextual analyses

5.1. Unilever's Feasible Sachets

Unilever, a worldwide shopper merchandise organization, has been effectively addressing natural worries connected with sachetization. They have presented sachets produced using reused plastics and have laid out assortment and reusing projects to advance feasible sachet use.

5.2. Refillable Sachets in Southeast Asia

In a few Southeast Asian nations, refillable sachets have acquired fame. Customers buy the underlying item in a sturdy sachet and afterward top off it at lower cost, decreasing single-use sachet squander.

6. Future Bearings and End

6.1. Reinforcing Reasonable Practices

Future economical sachetization drives should zero in on fortifying worldwide moral structures, improving responsibility systems, and expanding straightforwardness in supply chains.

6.2. Inclusivity and Strengthening

Endeavors ought to be made to guarantee that minimized networks, native people groups, and ladies are effectively associated with forming practical sachetization drives and profiting from them.

6.3. Maintainable Turn of events

Economical sachetization adds to more extensive maintainable improvement objectives, including mindful utilization and creation (SDG 12) and life underneath water (SDG 14). Progress toward these objectives ought to keep on being a focal point of worldwide endeavors.

6.4. Worldwide Coordinated effort

Tending to worldwide difficulties requires coordinated effort among legislatures, organizations, common society, and people. Economical sachetization drives give a stage to such cooperation

9.3 Global Governance in a Sashetized World

The sachetization peculiarity, portrayed by the bundling of shopper products in little, single-use sachets or parcels, has seen quick development around the world, especially in arising economies. While sachetization offers accommodation and reasonableness, it has likewise raised worries about its natural effect, administrative difficulties, and suggestions for worldwide administration. This exposition investigates the developing scene of worldwide administration in a sachetized world, underscoring the requirement for cooperative endeavors to address maintainability, exchange, and administrative issues in this unique setting.

1. **The Ascent of Sachetization**

   1.1. Sachetization as a Worldwide Pattern

   Sachetization has turned into a worldwide peculiarity, spreading over enterprises like food, individual consideration, and drugs. It takes special care of customers looking for reasonable, little amount items.

   1.2. Market Elements

   Arising economies, portrayed by different shopper inclinations and lower pay levels, have seen critical development in sachetized items because of their reasonableness and availability.

   1.3. Natural Worries

   The multiplication of sachets, frequently produced using non-biodegradable materials, has raised worries about plastic contamination, asset utilization, and waste administration.

2. **Maintainability Difficulties**

   2.1. Plastic Contamination

   The sachetization pattern has added to plastic contamination, with sachet bundling frequently winding up in landfills, seas, and biological systems, hurting natural life and the climate.

2.2. Asset Consumption

The development of single-use sachets consumes important assets, including oil based plastics and energy, compounding asset exhaustion and environmental change.

2.3. Shopper Conduct

Changing shopper conduct and inclinations toward manageable bundling present difficulties to sachetization-based organizations that should adjust to advancing customer requests.

3. **Worldwide Administration Contemplations**

3.1. Worldwide Exchange

Sachetization has prompted expanded worldwide exchange bundling materials, unrefined components, and sachetized items. Administrative harmonization and economic deals are basic to working with this exchange.

3.2. Ecological Guidelines

Worldwide administration bodies and shows, for example, the Basel Show and the Paris Understanding, assume a part in molding ecological guidelines and resolving plastic waste issues connected with sachetization.

3.3. Customer Insurance

Worldwide buyer insurance guidelines and associations should guarantee that sachetized items fulfill security and quality guidelines while tending to natural worries.

3.4. Reasonable Advancement Objectives (SDGs)

The Assembled Countries Manageable Improvement Objectives (SDGs), especially Objective 12 (Dependable Utilization and Creation), are integral to tending to supportability challenges related with sachetization.

4. **Open doors for Worldwide Administration**

4.1. Multilateral Arrangements

The advancement of multilateral arrangements and conventions can fit guidelines connected with sachetization, empowering feasible practices and mindful bundling.

4.2. Coordinated effort with Industry

Worldwide administration bodies can team up with sachetization businesses to lay out willful manageability norms and advance eco-accommodating bundling.

4.3. Examination and Information Sharing

Worldwide administration foundations can uphold examination and information assortment on the natural effect of sachetization, cultivating proof based policymaking.

4.4. Shopper Schooling

Worldwide administration bodies can work with states and industry partners to instruct customers about the ecological effect of sachetization and advance mindful utilization.

5. Contextual investigations

5.1. The European Association's Roundabout Economy Activity Plan

The European Association has done whatever it takes to decrease plastic waste and advance round economy standards. Drives, for example, the Single-Use Plastics Mandate mean to restrict the effect of sachetization on the climate.

5.2. ASEAN and Feasible Bundling

The Relationship of Southeast Asian Countries (ASEAN) has perceived the ecological effect of sachetization and started conversations on manageable bundling rehearses inside the area.

6. Challenges in Worldwide Administration

6.1. Administrative Abberations

Contrasts in guidelines and principles across nations and locales can make difficulties for worldwide administration endeavors to address sachetization-related issues.

6.2. Industry Interests

Industry campaigning and protection from guidelines might impede worldwide administration endeavors pointed toward advancing manageability in sachetization.

6.3. Authorization and Consistence

Guaranteeing consistence with guidelines and considering rebellious entertainers responsible can be trying in a globalized market.

6.4. Restricted Assets

Worldwide administration foundations might confront asset requirements, restricting their ability to resolve complex issues like sachetization.

7. Future Bearings and End

7.1. Embracing Economical Sachetization

The eventual fate of worldwide administration in a sachetized world relies on the reception of feasible sachetization rehearses that offset comfort with ecological obligation.

7.2. Administrative Harmonization

Endeavors to fit guidelines, advance maintainable bundling, and decrease plastic contamination ought to be vital for worldwide administration establishments.

7.3. Partner Commitment

Worldwide administration bodies ought to effectively draw in with states, industry partners, buyers, and common society to foster successful strategies and arrangements.

7.4. Training and Mindfulness

Teaching buyers about the ecological effect of sachetization and advancing mindful utilization is fundamental in driving change.

9.4 Predictions and Speculations

Forecasts and hypotheses are vital parts of human discernment and independent direction. From estimating the climate to expecting mechanical progressions, our capacity to foresee and hypothesize shapes how we might interpret the world and illuminates our decisions. Notwithstanding, the line between informed foreknowledge and unjustifiable guess can be foggy. In this paper, we will investigate the idea of forecasts and hypotheses, their jobs in different spaces, the difficulties they present, and the significance of decisive reasoning in exploring the unsure future.

1. **Forecasts: Reasonable Projections into What's in store**

   1.1. Logical Forecasts

   Logical forecasts are grounded in experimental proof, math, and thorough procedure. Fields like material science, cosmology, and climatology depend on prescient models to conjecture peculiarities like shrouds, weather conditions, and environmental change.

   1.2. Monetary Projections

   Financial analysts use information investigation and monetary models to make expectations about future financial circumstances, including Gross domestic product development, expansion rates, and joblessness rates.

   1.3. Innovative Progressions

   Forecasts about mechanical headways are in many cases in view of innovative work patterns, industry mastery, and logical forward leaps. These estimates educate the advancement regarding new innovations and businesses.

   1.4. General Wellbeing and Pandemics

   Disease transmission specialists and general wellbeing specialists make expectations about the spread of sicknesses in light of information examination, demonstrating, and verifiable examples, assisting states and medical care frameworks with getting ready for possible flare-ups.

2. **Theories: Informed Mystery with Vulnerability**

   2.1. Monetary Business sectors

   Examiners in monetary business sectors make ballpark estimations about the future execution of resources, for example, stocks and products, in light of market patterns, news, and financial pointers.

   2.2. Political Decisions

   Political examiners and savants hypothesize about political

decision results in light of surveying information, up-and-comer execution, and verifiable democratic examples.

2.3. Mechanical Futurism

Futurists take part in educated hypothesis about the future regarding innovation, imagining situations in view of current mechanical patterns and forward leaps.

2.4. Sci-fi

Sci-fi creators and makers utilize inventive hypotheses to investigate future prospects, frequently mixing science and innovativeness to imagine universes past our ongoing comprehension.

3. **Difficulties and Impediments**
3.1. Vulnerability

Expectations and hypotheses innately include vulnerability, as they endeavor to predict future occasions impacted by various factors, a large number of which are eccentric.

3.2. Inclination and Pomposity

Human mental inclinations, for example, tendency to look for predictable answers and carelessness, can prompt imperfect expectations and theories, as people will more often than not look for data that upholds their assumptions.

3.3. Deficient Data

Restricted or inadequate data can thwart the precision of forecasts and hypotheses, particularly while managing intricate, multi-layered issues.

3.4. Dark Swan Occasions

Dark swan occasions, uncommon and unanticipated events with huge effects, can upset even the most all around informed expectations and hypotheses.

4. **Significance of Decisive Reasoning**
4.1. Recognizing Expectations and Hypotheses

Decisive reasoning abilities assist people with separating between very much educated expectations supported by proof and simple hypotheses coming up short on a strong groundwork.

4.2. Assessing Source

Decisive reasoning includes examining the believability and mastery of sources giving expectations or hypotheses, which is pivotal for making informed decisions.

4.3. Taking into account Numerous Viewpoints

Drawing in with various perspectives and taking into account elective expectations and hypotheses can prompt a more exhaustive comprehension of a given issue.

4.4. Embracing Vulnerability

Decisive reasoning empowers an appreciation for vulnerability and intricacy, it are not reliable to perceive that expectations and hypotheses.

5. Moral Contemplations

5.1. Responsibility

Those making forecasts and hypotheses, especially in fields like general wellbeing or money, have a moral obligation to give straightforward and precise data.

5.2. Falsehood

Unreliable expectations and hypotheses can prompt deception and public disarray, highlighting the requirement for moral correspondence.

5.3. Staying away from Damage

Forecasts and hypotheses in regions like security and public wellbeing ought to focus on keeping away from hurt and potentially negative results.

6. The Job of Forecasts and Hypotheses In the public arena

6.1. Informed Navigation

Forecasts and hypotheses illuminate leaders in government, business, and the scholarly community, aiding key preparation and chance appraisal.

6.2. Logical Request

Expectations drive logical request by proposing speculations and hypotheses to be tried and approved through trial and error and perception.

6.3. Inventiveness and Investigation

Theories fuel innovativeness and investigation, moving craftsmen, essayists, and trend-setters to push limits and imagine novel fates.

6.4. Public Mindfulness

Forecasts and theories, when conveyed actually, raise public mindfulness about likely difficulties and potential open doors, empowering readiness and proactive reactions.